Here are touc true stories a and the stamps that commemorate them. You'll be entertained and amazed by tales about the French king who used playing cards for banknotes . . . about the governorship that was lost by one-sixth of a vote— the smallest margin in election history . . . about the country where you have to get a license to drive a reindeer and can be fined for driving one while drunk . . . about the military funeral that was held for an amputated leg.

These are tales of human intrigue and valor, stories garnered from around the world and throughout history. They all come from the man who's spent a lifetime pursuing strange or forgotten oddities of history—and of stamps.

Stories
Behind the
STAMP

by DOUG STORER

PUBLISHED BY POCKET BOOKS NEW YORK

AMAZING BUT TRUE STORIES
BEHIND THE STAMP

POCKET BOOK edition published November, 1976

ISBN: 0-671-80781-1.
Cover illustration by Howard Koslow.

Printed in the U.S.A.

To my wife, Hazel, without whose research and writing this book would not have been possible.

Contents

7

Introduction

ALTHOUGH I HAVE designed stamps for Turkey, Haiti, and Colombia, I am not a stamp collector. So it may seem strange that someone like me would write a book about stamps. But that is exactly what I've done.

You see, you don't have to collect stamps to be fascinated with them. I am a collector of stories, and behind every postage stamp there is a story—touching, bizarre, exciting, amazing.

My fascination with stamp stories goes back a long way, to the time I met a big, lively Australian who had acquired a very fine collection. His name was Captain Tim Healy and he'd served in British Intelligence during the First World War.

I remember well the first stamp story that Tim ever told me. I was to hear many more later, but this one held me spellbound.

"I had many experiences with stamps during the war," began Healy that first time. "I was a secret agent then and my chief job was nabbing spies. One day, when I was in London, I learned from the censorship department of Intelligence that they were watching very carefully the letters which a certain man was sending to Holland. The man was a stamp collector and was exchanging stamps with another collector in Amsterdam. It all seemed very innocent. The only reason they were reading his mail was because the letters were addressed to a house in Amsterdam where spies sometimes got their mail.

"Being a stamp collector myself," continued Healy, "I naturally was interested. I asked them to let me see the stamps the man was sending. For weeks, I studied these stamps and his letters. I could find nothing at all extraordinary about them.

"Then, suddenly, one day the thought flashed through my mind that perhaps the stamps themselves were a code. And sure enough, every stamp had a hidden meaning.

"The stamps he sent told a real story—secret information about the British army and navy. When he sent a two-shilling stamp to his friend in Holland, it meant that a battleship had just left England; a one-shilling stamp meant a cruiser; a five-penny stamp, a destroyer—and so on. When I had figured out this code, I caught my man!"

Captain Tim—who was a superb storyteller—had many stamp stories like this and I figured that others, like myself, would enjoy hearing them. So I put him on the air.

I was then head of radio for a New York advertising agency—the Blackman Company, now Compton. I had no difficulty in convincing a partner and account executive, Dick Compton, that a stamp program with Captain Tim as the narrator was a natural.

The program turned out to be a great success. Our client, Procter & Gamble, bought it and we named it the Ivory Stamp Club. It was aired twice a week for several years on a twenty-station network (NBC).

During the time the program was running, we gave away seven hundred million stamps and one and a quarter million albums in exchange for soap wrappers and money. That's a lot of soap, a lot of stamps—and a staggering record which has never been equaled.

The program proved to me that there are a lot of stamp collectors around—and a lot of people who like good stories.

So here's the book—with help from some stamp professionals like my good friend Clark Stevens of Belleair, Florida, and Bryant Le Duc, the St. Petersburg, Florida, stamp dealer who so kindly supplied most of the stamps used to illustrate the stories.

Doug Storer

President, Amazing But True, Inc.

The First Post Box

The first message left in the box was one of disaster.

IT'S A FAMILIAR sight. The blue-uniformed postman, his keys jingling from a long chain, opens the neighborhood post box and collects the mail. He bags it, swings it up on his truck and then is off to the central post office. Our letter is now on its way—perhaps to the farthest corner of the world.

The daily pickup and delivery of mail is, as someone has said, "an everyday minor miracle." But we are all used to it now and have long taken it for granted. Of course, that wasn't always so. Mail service could be a very chancy business, as we learn from the unusual story of the world's first post box, in the town of Mossel Bay, South Africa.

In 1500, Bartolomeu Dias, the great Portuguese explorer who discovered the Cape of Good Hope, drowned when his ship went down in a violent storm off the coast of South Africa. With Dias went most of his men and all but one of his ships. This vessel, which found shelter in the bay, safely rode out the storm. When the weather cleared the ship's captain prepared to sail homeward, putting the ill-fated expedition to an end.

Before leaving the bay, however, one of the ship's officers wrote out a detailed acount of the disaster and of the death of Dias. Then he put the letter in a shoe which he left hanging from a tree close to shore. The ship's officer hoped that someday, somehow, a European would find the letter and thus learn the tragic fate of the expedition. After all, it was a long way back to Portugal. If the surviving vessel did not make it, then there would be no record anywhere of the tragedy which had overtaken the explorer and his party.

A year later another Portuguese, a navigator named João da Nova who was in command of four ships on the way to India, also put in to Mossel Bay. He found the letter still in good condition deep inside the shoe, protected there from the ravages of both climate and insects. Da Nova built a little church at the bay (the first in South Africa) and a settlement of Europeans gradually grew up around it. From the first, the shoe—until it wore out—and the tree served as a post box for the growing colony and for the passing ships that came to the bay in increasing numbers.

Today the great ancient tree still stands at Mossel Bay, and the South African government has erected a monument beneath its spreading branches in honor of its use as the world's first post box.

The monument, with a plaque, is a concrete box. Its function is the usual one, for the deposit of mail. But its design is different from all others: it is in the form of an old Portuguese shoe.

"Collection Box"   U.S.A., 1973

A Vain Woman's Stamp

Wrong or not, insisted the governor's wife,
the stamps were to go out.

In 1847 THE little island of Mauritius, a British colony
in the Indian Ocean, still used the old-fashioned mail
service then common to most of the world: anyone with
a letter to mail took it to the post office, where a clerk
collected a fee and then marked the envelope "Post
Paid."

However, letters arriving in Mauritius from England
were then beginning to carry the just-invented postage
stamp, and the wife of the governor of Mauritius, Lady
Gomm, felt that their island should also go modern and
use the new stamp.

It was about this time that the governor was to give
a big fancy-dress ball, and Lady Gomm felt that it would

be a good idea to have stamps printed up in Mauritius and placed on the envelopes carrying the invitations.

The use of stamps, thought the lady, would make a great impression on all her fashionable friends, both on the island and abroad. Although her friends in England and Europe would not attend the ball in far-away Mauritius, Lady Gomm wanted them all to know she still followed a fashionable life style—even on her remote island.

The governor gave his wife permission to have the stamps made up, and Lady Gomm trotted down to the local jeweler, J. Barnard, with one of the new stamps she had recently received from England. The stamp bore the head in profile of Queen Victoria and, explained Lady Gomm, the jeweler was to engrave a Mauritius stamp just like it. Then the stamps were to be issued in one-penny and two-penny denominations.

Using the back of an old copper calling-card plate, Barnard made a faithful copy of the Queen's head for the center of the stamp. Then he engraved the words "Mauritius" along one side of the stamp and "Post Office" along the other. He never noticed in doing so that he had made a foolish error: the words opposite "Mauritius" should have been "Post Paid" and not "Post Office."

Finished with his engraving, the jeweler started to run off the stamps. Halfway through the printing, he became aware of his error and reported it to the governor.

At first, the decision was made to stop the run and destroy the stamps already printed. But the two men reckoned without Lady Gomm. She wanted her invitations to go out on time, and so the stamps—right or wrong—must be used. The governor, knowing his wife to be a determined woman, gave way to her pleas.

So the invitations went out bearing the flawed stamps.

Then, like most stamps, they were canceled and discarded along with the envelopes.

But a few of the stamps survived and today the Mauritius "Post Office" stamp—the result of a vain woman's insistence—is one of the most valuable in the world. The price for a used stamp is set at $55,000—the price of an unused one at $80,000.

"Post Office Stamp"   Mauritius, 1847

The Anthem—by Key, Congreve, and Smith

The new missiles had knocked out a city
. . . now they would be used against the
"colonies."

WITHOUT THE VERY different contributions of two now
forgotten Englishmen, Francis Scott Key would not
have written "The Star-Spangled Banner," the song
which grew out of the War of 1812 with England and
which finally became our national anthem by an act of
Congress.

One of these Englishmen was Sir William Congreve,
royal firemaster to the English court and chief planner
of fireworks for all kingly celebrations. Congreve ex-
celled at his calling, but he grew bored with its purely
festive limitations and set to work on something that he
figured would be more useful to his monarch and his
country.

Congreve's father was director of the Royal Arsenal
at Woolwich and there the firemaster was able to carry

on extensive experiments with gunpowder. At length he came up with a deadly invention, the war rocket which still bears his name.

That was in 1801. A year later, Congreve's invention was successfully used in a savage attack on Copenhagen. Under a fiery rain of twenty-five thousand British rockets, the Danish city was burnt to the ground. The next use made by the British of the Congreves was against the Americans in the War of 1812.

These early rockets were flimsy affairs, just narrow wooden tubes armed at the tips with iron warheads. Filled with gunpowder, they were fired from sharply tilted wooden troughs set up in rows so that a number of the missiles could be launched simultaneously in a single giant assault.

With a range of more than two miles, the rockets were designed to explode on impact, causing great destruction and striking terror into the hearts of all those who were unlucky enough to be on the field of battle when these amazing new missiles struck.

For its time, the rocket was a fearsome weapon, but it had one very bad defect. Its guidance system was extremely crude, consisting only of a long wooden pole set in the tail of the rocket to act as an uncertain rudder. As a result of this primitive control, much of the damage occasioned by Congreve's projectiles was not among the enemy troops, but among the British cannoneers. English soldiers often found themselves frantically dodging their own maverick rockets which, wobbling off course, would turn and home in on their dispatchers instead of on the enemy.

On the historic night of September 13 and the early morning of September 14, 1814, when the British fleet attacked Fort McHenry, near Baltimore, extensive use was made of the Congreve rockets. With their tails hissing and flaring as they streaked toward their target, followed by flaming explosions as they hit the fort, the rockets made a spectacular display. Over the harbor, the night sky was made brilliant with their eerie light.

This was the light which illuminated the scene of battle for Francis Scott Key, a young Washington lawyer who witnessed the fiery engagement from a British war-sloop on which he had been detained.

On the afternoon of September 13, Key had been taken to see the British admiral Cockburn. His mission was to secure the release of a dear friend, Dr. Beanes, a Maryland physician who was being held by the invading English on a charge of interfering with their troop movements.

Key was successful in his mission and was preparing to return upriver to Baltimore when he was told that the assault on Fort McHenry was about to start and that he would have to remain on the British ship until the fight was over. In short, he was a temporary prisoner.

All that night, as Key watched the pounding of the fort so gallantly defended by only a handful of men, his heart lifted each time he saw in the "rockets' red glare" the American flag still waving proudly above McHenry's ramparts.

Early the next morning the banner was still flying and Key, deeply moved, scribbled on the back of an old envelope the words which expressed his deep emotion at the sight of the flag above the beleaguered fort. These words were the first verse of "The Star-Spangled Banner."

While Congreve, the Englishman, was the source of the rockets which set the scene and the mood for our national anthem, it was another Englishman who provided the music.

When Francis Scott Key wrote his famous words he mentally set them to music. And the music he chose was the then very popular "To Anacreon in Heaven," which had originally been created as a lively English drinking song.

John Stafford Smith, a well-known eighteenth-century English conductor and organist, had composed the music. He had been asked to create a melody to fit the official poem of the Anacreontic Society of London. This was a club of gentlemen merrymakers which had been formed to pay homage to Anacreon, a Greek lyric poet who lived long before the Christian era and wrote torrid ballads about the delights of women and wine.

"To Anacreon in Heaven" first appeared in a collection of English songs which was published in London in 1783 under the title of *The Vocal Enchantress*. Eventually, the *Enchantress* found its way across the Atlantic and quickly charmed the hearts of American music lovers. Of all the music in the *Enchantress,* the London club's song became the most popular. Among its admirers was Francis Scott Key, the lawyer who sometimes wrote hymns and verses.

The words of "The Star-Spangled Banner" fit the difficult meter of "To Anacreon in Heaven" perfectly, and they clearly show that Key had the old drinking song in mind when he wrote his verses. To make certain, however, that his words would be sung to the proper melody, Key had a notation made on the first printing of the anthem that "To Anacreon In Heaven" was to be the "Tune."

To Sir William Congreve and John Stafford Smith, therefore, we owe a debt of gratitude. Without the contributions of these nearly forgotten Englishmen, we would not now be singing Francis Scott Key's stirring "Star-Spangled Banner," perhaps the best known and most dramatically conceived of all national anthems.

"Francis Scott Key"   U.S.A., 1948

The Great Party on the Nile

The pretty Empress didn't care for sight-seeing.

THE SUEZ CANAL was formally opened on November 17, 1869. In Cairo, Egypt's capital city, the event was marked by one of the most dazzling celebrations in history.

The great bash was put on by Ismail Pasha, then the khedive of Egypt and a man who believed that if you had it, you spent it. And Ismail had it.

As an expensive opener to the party, there was a guest list that numbered in the thousands. All of these, of course, were put up on the royal tab.

As might be expected of the friends of an absolute ruler, these guests were not of the beer-and-pretzels variety. The khedive was an international man, a charming sophisticate who spent much of his time in the capitals of Europe, where he found life congenial to his cultivated tastes. Those invited, therefore, were the titled, the rich, the famous, and the talented from all over the world.

To feed these high-level visitors, tons of delicacies were rushed to Egypt from all over the world, the perishables packed in costly ice. And to take care of their daily needs and comfort, fifteen hundred cooks, valets, and maids were imported from Europe to augment the local help.

Housing for the khedive's distinguished friends was of the most lavish kind, and no luxury or comfort was overlooked by the attentive host.

One guest was Eugénie, wife of Napoleon III, emperor of France. To make certain that the pretty young empress would feel royally at home during her short stay in Egypt, she and her huge retinue were put up in a glittering palace built just for her on the bank of the Nile.

The khedive went to great lengths to make this royal guest comfortable, but very little seemed to please Eugénie.

Pretty, witty, bored, and imperiously rude, the young empress was no Egyptologist and showed it. Whirled in splendor over a road built especially for the occasion, she was taken out on the desert to see the Great Pyramid of Cheops and the brooding, enigmatic Sphinx. Eugénie cast barely a glance at the ancient monuments, and made it clear she couldn't care less about sightseeing along the Nile.

Back in Cairo she proved a greater thorn to her host, purposely seeking as her temporary companions all those in disfavor with the khedive. Even her noble lady in waiting was shocked at the empress's conduct.

What the khedive privately thought of Eugénie's bad manners is not known.

The khedive did not overlook the matter of entertainment for his partying guests. To keep them happy during their stay in Egypt, Ismail Pasha had a magnificent new opera house built in Cairo. Then he commissioned Verdi, the Italian composer, to mark its opening with an original opera created around a North African theme.

The opera turned out to be the brilliant *Aïda*. But Verdi did not complete it in time for the grand opening, and the music lovers in the city on the Nile had to make do with the composer's *Rigoletto*. (Two years later, on December 24, 1871, the delayed opening of *Aïda* did take place in the Cairo Opera House.)

After the opening of the Suez Canal, the khedive continued on his extravagant way, spending more and more time abroad. Although he had several wives in Egypt, Ismail was not a man to ignore a pretty face. In Europe, he acquired a succession of lively mistresses and spent fortunes to maintain them in royal style.

In time, this high living, coupled with elaborate projects both at home and abroad, brought the khedive to the edge of bankruptcy. In 1875, facing financial ruin, he was finally forced to offer for sale Egypt's controlling shares in the Suez Canal.

Ironically, these shares were bought by England who, for years before the canal was built, had done everything possible to thwart the project. The English had been fearful then that the waterway would give the French, who built it, vast power in the Mideast, an area which England had already staked out as her own colonial preserve.

Now, by bailing out the khedive, England laid her fears to rest. With the khedive's shares, England bought herself a controlling interest in the passageway and was able to link her far-flung empire together by a quick and cheap water route that extended from the docks of London to the harbor of Hong Kong.

Today, however, England no longer controls the Suez. It is now back in the hands of the Egyptians, who seized the canal in 1956. (The Suez Canal stamp was issued that year to celebrate Egypt's victory.) Later, in the 1967 Arab–Israeli conflict, Egypt blocked all passage through the waterway by sending hundreds of ships to the canal's muddy bottom.

By a curious quirk of history, the Egyptians finally cleared the canal of sunken ships and opened it once again for traffic in 1975. That was exactly one century after Egypt lost the great waterway because of the free-wheeling spending of an extravagant ruler.

"Suez Canal"   *Egypt, 1956*

A Man for All Americans

He had only two years of schooling, but he's been called "the first genius born in the New World."

"BEN FRANKLIN," WROTE Balzac, the great French author, "should be credited with inventing the United States."

Well, he didn't quite do it all by himself, but as a superb statesman and diplomat, and as prime mover in the Continental Congress, the man who invented "Poor Richard" certainly left his indelible mark on our nation. And not only in politics.

Born in Boston on January 17, 1706, the seventh son of a poor soapmaker, Ben Franklin was apprenticed out to a printer at the age of ten, equipped with only two years of meager schooling.

But the boy loved learning for the sake of learning,

and young Ben taught himself so steadily and so well, and mastered so many subjects, that he was finally called the "most educated American of his time."

In his middle years, the universities of Yale, Harvard, and Oxford conferred honors on him in the field of science and philosophy. And Franklin could discuss these complex matters fluently in several languages—in French, Italian, Spanish, or Latin—all of which he had taught himself.

"It is the business of the future to be dangerous," Franklin said. And this belief was borne out by his hazardous experiments in kite-flying to establish the connection between lightning and electricity.

Franklin's sizzling experiments with his kite led to his invention of the lightning rod and the early storage battery, but they cost him many injuries and severe burns. Once, while trying to demonstrate the power of the terrible new force he had harnessed, Franklin attempted to electrocute a turkey. His experiment misfired and Ben, hurled senseless to the ground, was almost killed. When he regained consciousness, he observed ruefully that "instead of a turkey, I almost killed a goose."

People everywhere know of Franklin's most popular inventions—the mangle and the rocking chair, the stove which bears his name and the lively harmonica, the lightning rod and bifocal glasses. He even invented a surgical instrument for an operation performed on his brother.

But there are many other areas of daily living where we still benefit from the creative presence of this remarkable man.

It was Franklin's love of education that caused him to create the first circulating library and to help found the University of Pennsylvania. His love of pure scholarship also brought into being the still-prestigious American Philosophical Society.

Young Ben loved the sea and, later, he was the first to investigate and chart the mighty Gulf Stream, an accomplishment which changed the entire system of navigation along the Atlantic coast.

Civic life, believed the urbane Franklin, should be orderly and comfortable. So in his adopted city of Philadelphia he organized our first fire department and planned the first public hospital. He introduced paved streets and had them illuminated with smokeless street lights, the first of their kind. He also designed our nation's first public sanitation system, and our present system is still based on his method.

By the time he was eight years old, Franklin had taught himself not only to read but to write—and to write well. This skill remained his lifelong habit, and he exercised it continually. No one knows just how many letters, editorials, articles, and treatises this native American genius turned out during his long, busy eighty-four years. But it is known that more than sixteen thousand of his original manuscripts are in existence today.

As founder of the lively *General Magazine* and author of *Poor Richard's Almanack,* Franklin's fame as a publisher has carried right through to the present day.

Actually, Ben started his publishing career very early in life. When his brother was imprisoned for mocking public authority, sixteen-year-old Ben came to his rescue. Using the strange pen name of "Silence Dogwood," Franklin wrote and printed up a series of blistering attacks on public censorship.

In 1774, as publisher of the powerful *Pennsylvania Gazette,* Franklin created and printed the first American political cartoon. At that time Franklin was still anxious to preserve our union with England, so he had the cartoon drawn up as a warning to the mother country of what the consequences would be if she continued her oppressive acts against the American colonies. This historic cartoon was captioned: "Magna Britannia— Her Colonies Reduced." The figure representing Britain in the cartoon was that of a woman without arms or legs, sliding off the face of the world. It was a graphic message, but its meaning never got through to King George.

Ben's private life was a mixture of lively brilliance abroad (he captivated people everywhere with his charm, wit, and intellect) and sleepy peace at the hearthside. His wife was almost illiterate and rarely seen, but he was happy with this homespun woman, missed her when she died, and said of his forty-year marriage that it had been a good one and that "we throve together."

Only one deep sadness marred Franklin's fortunate life. His son, William Franklin, who was royal governor of New Jersey in 1776, did not agree with his father concerning the rightness of the revolution. William remained loyal to the Crown and worked in every way to thwart the aims of the embattled colonies. His hatred of the revolution grew so great that he sent a warning to say he "would kill three Americans for every British sympathizer who died." Branded finally as a spy and a traitor to the American cause, William's capture was ordered by the Revolutionary Congress of New Jersey. Hunted down and arrested, tried and convicted of treason, the royalist governor was sentenced to death. But because of the love and respect that the American people felt toward his patriot father, William Franklin's life was spared and he was sent to England in exchange for several American prisoners.

Among our native heroes, Franklin is always thought

of as the very finest symbol of the American character —or, at least, what we strive for ourselves to be.

Foremost among his many virtues was the strong American belief in the future. This trait of character was powerfully illustrated by Franklin when, as a very old man, he stood one day on a Paris street and with a French friend enthusiastically watched the ascension of an early balloon. The Frenchman, a skeptic, was unimpressed by the rare feat. "Of what earthly use is a balloon?" he asked. Franklin turned to the man with a smile. "Of what earthly use is a newborn baby?" the old wizard countered.

"Benjamin Franklin" U.S.A., 1956

The Greatest Sculpture the World Has Ever Seen

An argument put the faces of four Presidents on a mountain in South Dakota.

SITUATED IN THE lonely wind-swept Black Hills of South Dakota is the most fantastic monument of its kind in the world. It is carved into the face of craggy Mount Rushmore and has been called "the greatest sculptured project ever conceived and executed by man." Yet if it had not been for a disagreement between the artist and the sponsors of another mountain-carving project, Mount Rushmore might never have known the genius of its creator.

In 1916, forty-five-year-old John Gutzon de la Mothe Borglum, born in Idaho of Danish parents, was recognized as one of the nation's most respected sculptors. A product of art schools in San Francisco, Paris, and

London, he already had created a number of outstanding works which were famous in the United States. These included several likenesses of President Abraham Lincoln (one of which stands in the rotunda of the Capitol) and a series of figures of the Apostles in the Cathedral of St. John the Divine, in New York City.

But Gutzon Borglum, as he preferred to be known, long had dreamed of creating a massive masterpiece, and when the sponsors of a Confederate memorial for Stone Mountain, Georgia, came to him, he was ready to listen to their plan.

In the midst of World War I he began sketches for the massive work which would pay homage to the heroic struggle of the South during the Civil War. It was not until 1923 that work actually began. Then, before the project was well under way, Borglum and the sponsors of the undertaking began having a series of disagreements. In the weeks that followed, the dispute became more heated and, finally, Borglum resigned.

In the meantime, other dreamers, perhaps inspired by the Stone Mountain project, had begun thinking in terms of a huge national monument on the face of lonely Mount Rushmore. When Borglum became available, after his resignation from the Georgia project, the sponsors of the new monument asked for his assistance. The sculptor was only too happy to comply. Thus, in 1927, work began on one of the most colossal projects ever undertaken by a sculptor.

Mount Rushmore National Monument honors four of our greatest Presidents—George Washington, Thomas Jefferson, Abraham Lincoln, and Theodore Roosevelt.

The amazing work, which contains the giant likenesses of these four patriots, has been carved entirely out of the pale granite on the face of Mount Rushmore. The mountain is 6,000 feet above sea level and rises more than 500 feet above the valley floor which spreads out below. Each of the massive heads is more than 60 feet tall—twice the size of the head of the Sphinx of Egypt—and made to the scale of a man 465 feet tall.

Located about twenty-five miles from Rapid City, South Dakota, the entire sculpture is so brilliantly designed it can be seen clearly from as far away as sixty miles. The four massive heads cover an area of more than two square miles of the mountain's face.

Fittingly, the first figure, that of George Washington, was completed and the memorial officially dedicated on July 4, 1930. During the following eleven years, progress on the monument was sporadic; there were always new complications and a shortage of funds. But despite these handicaps, the stonecutters continued to chip away at the granite surface of the mountain, working from models made on the scale of one inch to one foot. Under the constant watchful eye of Borglum, the great heads slowly emerged from the stone.

Then, in 1941, with completion of the project in sight, Borglum, now seventy years old, died. Only a few final touches on the last figure, that of Roosevelt, remained. For these Borglum's son, Lincoln, a sculptor in his own right, stepped into his father's shoes, and the most mammoth sculpture ever created was finished.

So the dream of one of America's most talented sculptors was at last realized and Mount Rushmore took its rightful place as a part of our great national park system.

"Mount Rushmore"   *U.S.A., 1952*

The Unknowns

The fourth grave remains empty.

AT THE ELEVENTH hour on the eleventh day of the eleventh month of 1921 the body of the first unknown soldier was lowered into its simple marble crypt on a hillside in Arlington National Cemetery.

The time of the burial had been chosen to commemorate the exact hour and date on which the bugles of World War I had sounded their final "cease fire" in 1918. The armistice had been signed. The long and bloody struggle was over at last.

The "unknown" who was laid to rest in Arlington that day had been chosen in a ceremony that was simpler, but no less impressive, than the military observance which marked his final burial in the nation's capital.

Early in 1921, when the Tomb of the Unknown Soldier had been completed at Arlington, a much-decorated American sergeant, Edward Younger of the 59th Infantry, was selected by the military to choose the nameless hero who would occupy the tomb. Sergeant Younger was brought to the French town of Chalons-sur-Marne and taken to a small mortuary where, mounted on catafalques and watched over by a guard of honor, there stood four flag-draped military coffins.

The coffins contained the bodies of four unidentified men who had died in action during World War I. Their remains had been disinterred from the four American military cemeteries which are maintained in France at the battle sites of Belleau Woods, Thiaucourt, Bony, and Romagne.

Sergeant Younger was given a wreath of white roses and asked to single out by random choice any one of the four coffins. Younger prayed briefly and walked slowly past all the biers. Then, retracing his steps, he paused before the second coffin and placed the fragrant flowers on top of the covering flag. The first Unknown Soldier had been chosen.

The body was brought home from Europe on the navy cruiser *Olympia,* which had been dispatched just for this escort purpose.

After its arrival in Washington, the body of the "unknown" lay in state under the great dome of the Capitol's Rotunda. Then, with as solemn honors as were ever given any military hero, the soldier nobody knew was placed in his final grave.

Although the war in which he gave his life was meant to end war for all time, our first Unknown Soldier was not to lie alone for very long. In 1958, on Memorial Day, he was joined in his crypt by two more nameless heroes, casualties of World War II and the Korean War.

Early in that year, the bodies of thirteen unidentified

men killed in World War II were brought to Epinal, France. These bodies had been disinterred, one each from the thirteen American military cemeteries in Europe and Africa, and represented all the men who had died in the Western theater of the war. The choice among these thirteen "unknowns" was made by General Edward O'Neil who, walking among the coffins, placed a wreath of red and white flowers on one of them.

Meanwhile in Honolulu, at the same time and by the same process, the body of an "unknown" who had died in the Pacific during World War II was also chosen, along with that of an "unknown" from the Korean conflict.

The selection of the Korean War "unknown" was made final in Honolulu, but a choice now had to be made between the two "unknowns" of World War II, each of whom had died in a different theater of that war, one in the Pacific and the other in the Europe–Africa area.

This choice was made at sea. The body chosen at Epinal was borne home on the destroyer *Blandy*. The two from Hawaii were carried together on the cruiser *Boston*. Off the Virginia Capes the two ships rendezvoused with the *Canberra* and a sea-transfer of the three bodies was made to the latter vessel. Aboard the *Canberra* the two coffins from World War II were stripped of all signs indicating from which theater of war they'd come, thus making the places where the men had fallen as anonymous as their names.

The honor of making the final choice between the two World War II "unknowns" now fell to the lot of navy hospitalman William Charette, himself a medal of honor winner. Charette made his solemn decision in the same manner as had his predecessors, by placing a wreath of flowers on one of the two coffins. Later the body of the second World War II "unknown," the one not chosen for the Tomb, was committed to the sea, accompanied by prayers from the chaplains of four different faiths.

The two remaining bronze coffins (holding the bodies of the final unknowns from World War II and Korea) were then brought to Washington. There they lay in state at the Capitol as tens of thousands passed before their biers in silent homage or wracking grief. Under the soft fabric of the flag, beneath the unyielding metal, lay someone's father or son, husband or brother.

Side by side below the high dome of the Rotunda, the two nameless warriors, home at last, waited for the slow-rolling caissons, the black-plumed horses, the muffled drums that would take them to rest forever beside their older comrade-at-arms on the gentle hillside at Arlington.

Since those two burials in 1958, a fourth crypt has been prepared at Arlington for still another "unknown." But this grave will probably always remain empty. So far, not a single unidentified body has come out of the tragic Vietnam War.

"Arlington Amphitheatre" U.S.A., 1922

Praying Hands

It's just a detail in a church painting, but it is revered throughout the world.

ALBRECHT DÜRER IS Germany's foremost painter. His great canvases—such as his *Venetian Woman* and *Portrait of a Young Man*—hang in prestigious museums throughout the world and bring staggering sums when sold.

But Dürer's masterpiece, the work by which he is best known, is not one of his most famous paintings. It is just a detail in a larger canvas.

Dürer was one of eighteen children born to a goldsmith in Nuremberg, Germany, in 1471. He was apprenticed early in his father's craft, but showed no inclination to pursue it. Painting was his goal in life. At the age of fourteen, when he painted a fine portrait of the Virgin Mary, his father finally agreed that the boy should follow his calling.

Young Albrecht was sent to study under a master painter of his time. He did well and five years later went off on his own.

Times were hard for everyone then, and especially for a poor, unknown artist. So Dürer and another artist friend pooled their resources, rented a studio, and commenced to live and paint together.

Neither made much progress, but it was soon apparent that Dürer was a far better artist than his friend. So the friend decided that he would go to work and earn the money needed to support them both. This would allow Dürer to continue his painting undisturbed by financial worries. Later, when money started coming in from Albrecht's paintings, his friend would resume his own career.

Albrecht agreed, and his friend went out daily to work long hours as a goldsmith, a craft which he had learned previously. It was a selfless gesture and Dürer, keenly aware of the sacrifices made on his behalf, worked furiously to succeed at his art.

It took time, but finally Dürer was successful and there was enough money coming in from his work to support both men. Now his friend could leave his goldsmith's bench and return to the studio and the easel he had abandoned for so long.

But it wasn't any good; the man found he could no longer paint. Tragically, the long period of hard work he had put in as a goldsmith, the prolonged use of sharp tools and hot metals, had damaged his sensitive hands. He was no longer capable of holding a brush, of doing any work of consequence.

One day shortly after the acknowledgment of defeat by his friend, Dürer entered the studio and found the saddened man kneeling before a window, his uplifted hands folded in prayer.

The sight inspired Dürer. He had just been commissioned to do an altar painting for a church in the town of Heller. The subject of the painting was to be the death of the Virgin Mary, and one of the Apostles surrounding her was to be shown kneeling in prayer—just like Dürer's friend.

The artist moved quickly. Asking the man not to stir from his position, Dürer rapidly made a sketch of the kneeling figure, paying particular attention to the work-worn hands.

The painting incorporating this detail was finally completed, accepted, and hung in the obscure little church for which it had been commissioned. There it stayed, unnoticed, for almost four hundred years. Then, around the turn of the century, the picture was discovered and bought by the Albertine Museum in Vienna.

Soon after this, a young Austrian art student working in the museum was struck by the praying hands in Dürer's old church canvas and made a faithful sketch of them. This was published in a magazine, and suddenly the hands were famous: everyone wanted a copy of them.

The appeal of the painting lies in the nature of the hands. They are shown scarred by years of toil. Yet they have about them an almost mystical beauty. Folded in humble prayer, they awaken a reverence in the viewer such as no lofty religious canvas can ever do. They touch the heart and the spirit of man. For they *are* man, that enduring creature of hardship and hope.

Dürer's painting of the hands of his selfless, obscure friend (no one knows his name) has immortalized the man and made Dürer more famous. Today, the "Praying Hands" is one of the most reproduced works of art in the world.

"Praying Hands"   Canada, 1966

Birth Certificate of a Nation

Should we really celebrate our freedom
on the Fourth of July?

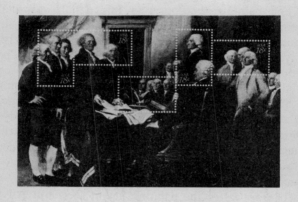

EACH YEAR WE cheer as cannons boom, flags fly, and
oratory flows in honor of our great and glorious Day of
Independence. Yet our independence was not decided
upon, voted for, signed into being, nor even proclaimed
on the Fourth of July. Many historians say that we are
celebrating the wrong day, but no one knows quite why.

The first move for American Independence was made
on June 7, 1776, when Richard Henry Lee, delegate
from Virginia, stood before his fellow members of the
Continental Congress, assembled in Philadelphia, and
formally demanded a complete break with England.

Lee's plea was not adopted then, but it gained increasing support and on July 2 a motion for indepen-

dence was passed by the Congress without a single dissenting vote. On that day, our ties with England were severed forever.

Immediately following this vote, John Adams—delegate from Massachusetts and a future president of the just-born nation—sent a letter to his wife, Abigail, in Boston. He wrote:

> The second day of July, 1776, will be the most memorable [in] the History of America . . . It ought to be commemorated as the Day of Deliverance [and] be solemnized with Pomp and Parade, with Shews, Games, Sports, Guns, Bells, Bonfires . . . from this Time forward forever more.

The Philadelphia *Evening Post* shared Adams's view of the date and on July 2, 1776, reported: "This Day the Continental Congress declared the United States free and independent."

Two days later, on July fourth, the delegates met for one matter of business only: to agree on the exact wording of the Declaration of Independence, which had been drawn up by Thomas Jefferson.

With minor changes, the Declaration was found satisfactory, but the actual signing of the official document did not take place until four weeks later, on August 2, 1776. Most members of the Continental Congress signed that day, but several were not present at the time and signed later.

The last man to put his signature on the Declaration was Thomas McKean, a delegate from Delaware. McKean had voted for independence on July second but then had galloped off at once to aid George Washington's badly battered forces. Kept busy by the Revolutionary War, McKean was not able to sign the historic document—and make it officially complete—until 1781.

The men who signed the Declaration of Independence were all men of substance—landowners, merchants, lawyers, college presidents. One of them, Benjamin Rush, was a doctor who later founded Dickinson College.

The signers were also a clannish group: of the fifty-six delegates, one quarter were related to each other. The wealthy Lees of Virginia were brothers. The two Adamses from Massachusetts were cousins, as were also New York's Lewis and Livingston. In addition, Lewis was also related to Harrison, a delegate from Virginia. Pennsylvania's Ross was brother-in-law to Delaware's Read. Brothers-in-law, too, were Middleton and Rutledge, both from South Carolina. (Rutledge was also, at twenty-seven, the Declaration's youngest signer.) There was even a father-and-son-in-law duo, Stockton of New Jersey and young Dr. Rush.

The signers of the historic document all took their lives in their hands, and they knew it. In the eyes of the English crown, they were subjects who were committing high treason, a crime which was then, as now, punishable by death.

Thomas Jefferson expressed the thoughts of many delegates when he said that some of them might be "exalted on a high gallows." To guard against this, the names of the signers were kept secret for a year. Although none of the signers was hanged, many paid dearly for their dedication to freedom, and some even paid with their lives.

Lewis Morris, a signer from New York, was impoverished by the Revolution. He suffered a long exile from his beloved Bronx estate and returned to find it in ruins. His health broken by shock and grief, he lived out his days in quiet resignation.

Thomas Nelson, a wealthy signer from Virginia, poured his entire estate into the cause for independence and died in utter poverty. He is buried in an unmarked pauper's grave at Yorktown, Virginia.

The Revolution cost old Ben Franklin his son, William. A former governor of the New Jersey colony, William turned royalist spy and was sentenced to death after his capture by the Revolutionary forces. But because of the deep public respect the colonists had for his patriotic father, William's sentence was commuted to deportation to England.

Francis Lewis, another signer from New York, lost his home, which was burned to the ground by the king's soldiers. He also lost his wife. She was imprisoned by the British and treated so badly that she died from the effects.

When Caesar Rodney put his signature on the Declaration, he knew that he was signing his life away. For some time Rodney had been suffering from a spreading malignancy which impaired his health and was now beginning to show on his face. He could not be treated in the colonies, only in England. As a private citizen Rodney could have gone to London for the needed treatment of his cancer. But as a "traitor"—a signer of the Declaration—England was closed to him. In the end, Rodney died in agony, his face so disfigured that he covered it with a heavy green veil during the final months of his life.

Richard Stockton, a scholar who signed for New Jersey, died brokenhearted during his long imprisonment by the British, who upon capturing him put the torch to his beloved library, one of the finest in the country. While it burned to the ground, Stockton was forced to stand by and watch.

Button Gwinnett of Georgia and Thomas Lynch of South Carolina were two signers whose deaths were caused indirectly by the Declaration and the war which followed it. Gwinnett, because of his political activities in the Continental Congress, was made commander in chief of his state's army. An abortive campaign to take Florida from the British brought him searing criticism from General Lachlan McIntosh. A public insult followed and resulted in a duel during which Gwinnett was killed.

Thomas Lynch, who was in very bad health when he signed, was advised to seek the warm climate of southern France. Because of the Revolution, which he had helped to bring about, Lynch could not sail directly for France as England controlled the seas and was on the lookout for all traitors. To avoid capture, Lynch slipped out of the country on a small boat bound for the Dutch-held island of Saint Eustatius, in the Caribbean. It was his intention to get another ship from there, but he never reached the island. His ship ran into heavy weather not long after sailing and went down with all hands.

The last draft of the Declaration of Independence was also a casualty of the times. When Thomas Jefferson presented his copy of the Declaration to Congress on July fourth, the members made a number of changes before approving it for publication. Jefferson then went back to his desk and wrote out a new "fair copy"— as he put it—reflecting these changes. This was the final draft of the Declaration, with the wording as we know it today. John Hancock, as president of the Continental Congress, and John Thompson, as secretary, signed this final copy. It was then sent to a Philadelphia printer, John Dunlap, to be set up in type for broadsides. These posterlike sheets were to be distributed throughout the colonies by courier to advise the people that they were now free of the English yoke.

The broadsides were delivered, all right, but the copy of the Declaration from which they had been made was not returned. Nor has it ever been seen since. To this day, its disappearance remains a mystery. Of course, if it is ever found, it will be the most valuable political document in American history. Think of it—the final draft of the Declaration of Independence, written in Jefferson's own hand and signed by John Hancock!

And what of the copy of the Declaration which is now enshrined in Washington? Well, the men of the Continental Congress were well aware that what they had done on that hot July day would have great historical significance. So in secret session on July 19, 1776, they voted to have the Declaration "fairly engrossed on parchment" by a fine professional penman named Timothy Matlack. This, they resolved, would be signed by all fifty-six delegates and become the new nation's official and permanent testament to its independence.

And so it has. This is the parchment copy which is now kept under heavy security in the National Archives Building in Washington. Through a thick shield of bullet-proof glass, it is viewed annually by millions of Americans whose freedom is forever secured to them by this noble document written two centuries ago.

"Declaration of Independence" U.S.A., *1976*

The Pacific Holds Her Secret

The flight was going well, and then . . .
silence.

"SHE BELIEVED STRONGLY that women should win their own way and not be given any special consideration, economically or physically."

That was the way Mrs. Muriel Morrissey, sister of the dauntless Amelia Earhart, described the flyer shortly after her death in 1937, a death which remains shrouded in mystery but which many believe occurred in service to her country.

Amelia Earhart was born in Atchison, Kansas, in 1897, just six years before the Wright brothers successfully performed the first heavier-than-air flight at Kitty Hawk, North Carolina. Certainly there is no reason to believe that she was exposed to flying any time in the years immediately after that event. But it appears she began developing her attitudes toward life and the role of women during those formative years.

For example, among her personal effects, which were made public after her death, was a scrapbook which she had begun assembling at an early age. Contained in it were newspaper clippings which cited the accomplishments of women from all over the world. Many bore little handwritten notes of congratulations from the girl who would make headlines of her own as a woman.

About the time she graduated from high school, World War I engulfed the world. Amelia went east to offer her services in helping to care for wounded American soldiers who were then returning to this country. Among them were many flyers, and the tales they told began to stir an interest in aviation in the restless young woman. When the war ended, however, her parents insisted that she resume her education and she enrolled in New York's Columbia University.

But the flying bug had bitten her, and campus life seemed trivial by comparison. So she soon dropped out of school and went to California, seeking a job which would pay for flying lessons. In the next couple of years she obtained her license but, unable to find a flying job on the West Coast, returned east, hoping that her luck would change. Again, such jobs were almost impossible to find for women, so Amelia took a job as a social worker in Boston, hoping something in aviation eventually would come her way.

Nothing permanent offered itself, but Amelia continued to fly at every opportunity and soon she was being recognized as one of the leading women pilots in the nation.

Finally, in 1928, less than a year after Charles Lindbergh had flown solo across the Atlantic Ocean, Amelia Earhart got her big break. She was selected to be a passenger—the first woman so honored—on a trans-atlantic flight. Later she would say of the trip, "The bravest thing I did was to drop a bag of oranges and a note on the head of an ocean liner's captain."

Nevertheless, her fame now was established. In the years that followed, she became an international celebrity and wrote a chapter in aviation history such as few women have been able to equal.

In 1932, she flew the Atlantic alone, from Harbor Grace, Newfoundland, to Ireland. In 1935, she soloed from Hawaii to California and, shortly thereafter, became the first person to fly alone across the United States in both directions.

In 1937, she announced that she and her navigator, Fred Noonan, would attempt a 27,000-mile flight around the world. On June 1, Earhart and Noonan took off from Miami Municipal Airport on that remarkable journey. Aviation enthusiasts around the world followed the daily accounts that traced the route of this beloved flyer. Then, in July, newspaper headlines announced that radio contact with the pair had been lost. Up until then, the flight had been going well. Months passed and silence continued to blanket the disappearance. Every search proved useless, and the whole world speculated about the fate of the two flyers. Then World War II intervened, and Amelia Earhart became but a memory.

But the story was not yet over.

After the war, new light was thrown on the subject. Servicemen returning from the Pacific theater claimed they had discovered the fate of this intrepid woman. According to their stories, Earhart had made a forced landing on a small, remote island in the Pacific. There, she and Noonan had been captured by the Japanese, who were then preparing to go to war. Both of the flyers, according to these accounts, had been executed as spies.

What actually happened has never been revealed officially, but the memory of Amelia Earhart, one of this nation's foremost pioneer aviators, lives on, her fame assured. If the spy story is true, she gave her life in defense of her country as surely as the thousands of combat personnel who fell on the battlefields. If it is not, her fame is no less diminished.

"Amelia Earhart" U.S.A., 1963

Spaceship—1492

A flock of birds prevented a mutiny and kept the ship sailing on.

IT WASN'T BY chance that Apollo 11, our first moonship, was named *Columbia.*

That name was chosen to honor the spirit of "adventure, exploration, and seriousness" with which Columbus embarked on his first dangerous voyage to the unknown New World almost five centuries ago.

The men who accomplished both these feats of exploration were all alike in their cool intelligence and incredible courage. But what a difference in the ships that carried them to their historic goals.

Columbus's little flagship, the *Santa Maria,* would have looked like a toy beside the towering 36-story-high Saturn rocket that launched the spaceship. Weighing a mere 110 tons, the little wooden ship measured a short 80 feet from stem to stern and was only 25 feet wide at her beam.

Columbus, like the astronauts, helped design his famous ship and was familiar with every detail of its construction. Daily he pored over the ship's plans, the originals of which may still be seen in a Barcelona museum.

Finally, after a total outlay of only $15,000 (less than the cost of a single space suit) the *Santa Maria* was ready. On August 3, 1492, with the great navigator on her bridge, the little flagship—the *Niña* and *Pinta* in her wake—sailed out of the sunny harbor of Palos and started on the voyage that would change the world.

Other mariners in Columbus's time believed that the world was round, as the ancient Greeks had said. But no one had ever tried to prove it. It was too dangerous. If it wasn't round and a ship went over the earth's edge, it could never sail back up again.

It was believed there were other hazards, too. Fantastic monsters, it was said, lived in the depths of the far-off seas which were dotted with islands inhabited by hostile beings, dog faced and one eyed.

Columbus was certain, however, that he would overcome any dangers and reach India by a new water passage. He took along an interpreter to speak with the Grand Khan, letters of greeting from Queen Isabella, and his most impressive official robe, made of red velvet and trimmed with white ermine. It was to be a very dignified first meeting. (There is no record of what the American Indians thought when they first saw this brilliant, and very warm, apparel.)

A surgeon sailed with Columbus. He took care of the crew's frequent injuries and treated any illness with massive doses of purgatives, herbal tinctures, and garlic. He also carried limes along to treat scurvy, although the connection between the disease and citrus was only dimly understood in those days.

Like the crew of Apollo 11, the men on the *Santa Maria* were kept endlessly busy. The many sails and the miles of rigging had to be tended night and day. Watches had to be stood and the heavy tiller manned, the long periods of work measured by a giant hourglass. Hot pitch had to be constantly applied to keep the wooden decks from rotting. And heavy seas and bad storms brought serious damage that had to be tediously repaired. The work never stopped.

Columbus's sailors slept whenever they could; they had no regular hours. In fair weather they slept on deck, in foul they huddled in the fetid darkness of the crew's quarters. Clothes were never removed; the men slept wrapped in the heavy hooded smocks that all sailors then wore.

Unlike the astronauts, Columbus's men had no problem about removing heavy boots: they had none. Their bare feet had hard, calloused soles, as protective as any leather, and their strong toes were as flexible as fingers from long years of swarming up swaying masts.

Like the dehydrated food carried in a spacecraft, the food aboard the *Santa Maria* could be summed up in one word: monotonous. The men had one big meal a day, around noon. This was basically beans and rice. To this plain fare were frequently added dried salt pork, beef, and fish, along with cheese and nuts. The menu was heavy on protein, with honey and raisins used for sweets. There was one gastronomical treat, though. Everything was washed down with good Spanish wine.

The "stove" on the *Santa Maria* was a hot bed of charcoal laid in a sandbox surrounded by buckets of water. As in a spacecraft, fire was the greatest danger aboard the little wooden vessel.

The men on the *Santa Maria* were treated well by fifteenth-century standards, which were brutally harsh on seamen. Thanks to Columbus's treatment of them, not a single man in his crew got sick or died on the long voyage to the New World. Columbus, a good captain and far ahead of his time, believed that psychology was far more effective than force. He meted out no punishment—not even when, near the end of the voyage but with land still unseen, his men threatened to mutiny unless he turned back. Columbus knew that his sailors were frightened by the lonely, endless sea, so he promised that if they didn't find land in another day or two, he'd do as they demanded. The following day, as if by a miracle, a flight of land birds winged past the *Santa Maria* and the mutiny was forgotten in wild anticipation of making a landfall.

Similar in many ways as the voyages of the *Santa Maria* and Apollo 11 were, there was one final great difference between them: after accomplishing its mission, the moonship returned home in triumph. The little wooden ship did not. After Columbus landed at San Salvador on October 12, 1492, and claimed all the New World for the Spanish throne, he lifted anchor and sailed on down the Caribbean. On Christmas Eve, while cruising off the coast of Haiti, the *Santa Maria* ran aground and was wrecked. Her great mission accomplished, the valiant little ship sailed no more.

"The Santa Maria"   *Spain, 1930*

They Rode As If Demons Pursued Them

The word was: the mail must go through.
And men like Buffalo Bill carried it.

THE ADVERTISEMENT APPEARED in many Western papers. It was short and to the point. It read:

Wanted, young skinny wiry fellows not over eighteen. Must be expert riders, willing to take risks daily. Orphans preferred. Wages $25.00 per week.

The advertised job doesn't seem like much now—no fringe benefits like a good pension plan, use of the company's credit card, a month's vacation. And as for the wages? Come off it!

But that job had a lot of takers in its day. Not only was the pay good for that time, but the skinny kids who applied for it, if they were lucky, got to ride the wind as heroes of the hour. They would be Pony Express men.

The Pony Express was inaugurated on April 3, 1860, in an effort to shorten the time it took to transport mail from St. Joseph, Missouri, to California. Previously the postal service had been supplied by stagecoaches rolling over a long southern route which often took three weeks or more to complete. But because of the tensions which gripped the nation as it crept closer and closer to the Civil War, West Coast residents began demanding faster service.

Led by California Senator William M. Gwin, a group of promoters joined together to found the new service and establish a shorter central route, which they felt would help solve the problem. By establishing a series of relay stations every ten to fifteen miles along a selected route, they were able to cut more than one hundred miles from the old line.

The route followed the Platte River through Nebraska, traversed South Pass in Wyoming, swung south of the Great Salt Lake, made its way across the salt desert to Carson City, Nevada, and then across the Sierra Nevada to Sacramento, California. From Sacramento the mail was loaded aboard river steamers and sent on to San Francisco. Mail arriving at either terminal was packed into rainproof leather pouches and handed to daring riders who dashed off for the next relay station.

As each Pony Express man arrived at a station he would pull his mail pouch from his saddle, jump down from his tired horse, leap on a fresh mount, and then take off again at top speed. He would repeat this at every way station until he had traveled seventy-five whirlwind miles, at which point the exhausted rider, as well as his horse, would be replaced by a fresh rider.

As soon as this man had received the mail pouch, he would continue the journey at a gallop.

Although each rider usually covered only the assigned 75 miles of the nearly 2,000-mile distance, combined they moved the mail at an average of approximately 250 miles per day.

The total load seldom weighed more than twenty pounds and the charge to customers, at the beginning of the service, was five dollars per half ounce. As the system improved, however, that cost was lowered to one dollar per half ounce.

Not only did the exposed riders have to cope with all kinds of weather, they also faced hostile Indians and bandits. But despite these dangers, the Pony Express established an almost unbelievable record of losing the mail only once during its lifetime, a lifetime which covered more than 650,000 miles of travel.

The fastest trip ever recorded during the brief history of the service was on a route between Fort Kearney, Nebraska, and Fort Churchill, Nevada, in November, 1860. On that trip, which was completed in the amazing time of just six days, riders carried the news of Abraham Lincoln's election as President.

During its brief and hectic period of life, the Pony Express employed more than 80 riders and 400 station keepers and assistants. It maintained 190 relay stations and more than 400 first-class horses. The riders usually were paid between $100 and $150 per month, high wages for those days. It attracted such Western heroes as Buffalo Bill Cody.

But just as the demand for more speed had fathered the birth of the famed service, so did the same demand spell its death. Late in 1861, the intercontinental telegraph line was completed across the plains and the need for the Pony Express ended. On October 24, 1861, eighteen months and twenty-one days after the first rider raced off from St. Joseph, the service was suspended.

One of the most colorful eras in the nation's history was over.

Had it been worth the effort?

The slogan of the Pony Express was "The Mail Must Go Through." Thanks to the brave men who rode the dangerous route, it did. Best of all, it went through faster than ever before. And this speedy new means of communication was one of the greatest factors in the opening of the Far West to trade and commerce.

"Pony Express"   *U.S.A., 1960*

The Return of a Hero's Body

For more than a century he lay in an un-marked grave in France.

THE REVOLUTIONARY WAR had two naval heroes, Scottish-born John Paul Jones and Irish-born John Barry. But it was the fate of Jones to venture more boldly, fight more brilliantly, live more splendidly, and die more tragically than Barry. So, of the two men, it is John Paul Jones we remember best. In the nation he served so well, his memory is kept forever green, and many call him the Father of the American Navy.

The war sloop *Ranger,* fresh from the Portsmouth navy yard, was put under Jones's command in 1777. Prowling the English Channel months later (in April, 1778), Jones met and defeated the *Drake,* a big British frigate. Barry had previously seized a British tender, but Jones's victory marked the first time an enemy man-of-war had surrendered to the Continental navy.

But this triumph over the *Drake* was not Jones's finest hour; that came the following year. Late in the evening of September 23, 1779, while cruising off the coast of England in another vessel, the *Bonhomme Richard* (a creaky old tub literally put together from spare parts), Jones spied an enemy convoy sailing home to London from the Baltic. Leading the convoy was the great British warship, the *Serapis*. Although totally outclassed by this English giant, Jones immediately waylaid and attacked the enemy vessel. To this day, this unequal engagement remains the most fantastic single ship action in all naval history.

The battle between the *Serapis* and the *Bonhomme Richard* was fought at night, under a rising full moon. During the four hours for which it thundered on, the poorly equipped American ship took a savage beating. The superior armament of the British frigate steadily raked the smaller vessel and, within an hour after the attack started, the *Richard* was in deep trouble. The enemy guns had knocked out her main cannon, splintered her rigging, and set her afire with flaming shot. Her hull had been breached in several places and was leaking badly. On her ravaged deck, half her crew lay dead or wounded.

It was then—against seemingly impossible odds—that Jones executed one of the boldest maneuvers in all the annals of naval warfare. Knowing that he could not survive the battering of the *Serapis*'s long-range guns, he decided that he would make the guns useless by taking the fight up close, right to the deck of the enemy ship.

So Jones closed in on the big Britisher. Under a punishing rain of shot, Jones brought the disabled *Richard* alongside the *Serapis,* threw grappling hooks aboard, and succeeded in lashing the two vessels together, starboard to starboard.

From his bridge, the English captain could not believe what he was seeing. Jones must be mad. Surely he did not think he could storm the warship from the burning, sinking *Richard?* The whole operation had been foolhardy from the start. Only one way out remained; Jones must call quits.

Across the narrow space that now separated them, the captain of the *Serapis* hailed Jones: "Do you surrender?" he shouted. Immediately Jones's answer came back. Out of the night, out of the fire and smoke and noise of battle, came the immortal words: "I have not yet begun to fight."

And Jones meant it! A few minutes later, with his remaining crew behind him, he leaped from the doomed *Richard* to the deck of the *Serapis*. It was a daring, go-for-broke effort—and it worked. Against all rational odds, John Paul Jones and his handful of valiant men overran the mighty British warship and took her captive. It was a victory for the ages.

Everywhere, during the Revolutionary War, Jones was feted as a hero. But heroes have a way of being abandoned once the smoke of battle clears, and that's how it was with John Paul Jones. Neglected by his countrymen, he died alone and in obscurity in a Paris rooming house on July 18, 1792. He was only forty-five years old. There were no claimants for the body of the man who had once been wildly cheered as our new nation's foremost naval hero. His burial in Paris, in the Protestant cemetery of St. Louis, was attended by only a handful of mourning friends.

One of these was a Frenchman named Pierre Simmoneau, a man who believed that someday the United States would remember its fallen hero and want Jones's body returned for the honorable interment it deserved.

So Simmoneau, footing all the funeral expenses, had Jones placed in a heavy lead coffin which was then flooded with alcohol and tightly sealed. This, Simmoneau felt, would help preserve the body for future recognition.

But Jones's body was not claimed during Simmoneau's lifetime and eventually, after the Frenchman's death, even the location of Jones's grave was lost.

Then in 1899 Horace Porter became our ambassador to France. From his earliest childhood, Porter had been a navy buff and John Paul Jones had been his greatest hero. The fact that Jones had never been properly honored had always disturbed Porter. Now, as he would be living in France—and had great personal wealth—he determined to find his hero's burial place and have Jones accorded the posthumous recognition he deserved.

The search for Jones's body was long, difficult, and costly, but in 1905 Porter's efforts were rewarded. The body of Jones was found under the earthen floor in the cellar of an old house. The cemetery of St. Louis had originally been on the outskirts of Paris, but the growing city had long before overrun the old burial place and most of the graves had disappeared beneath the dwelling sites. The diggers, under Porter's guidance, had unearthed five lead coffins from the same area. Three of these bore French name plates, and the fourth was that of a man over six feet tall. Clearly, this could not be the coffin of Jones, who was small in stature.

When the fifth coffin was prized open, however, there was no doubt about the body it contained. Thanks to the preserving alcohol supplied by the faithful Simmoneau, it was possible to positively identify the lost hero's remains. Jones's identity was further certified by known measurements of the skull and body of the dead man, by comparing his cast of features and hair coloring with those shown in old paintings, and even by the condition of the preserved kidneys. These revealed an advanced case of nephritis, the disease for which Jones had been treated and from which it was known he had died.

The discovery of Jones's body created a storm of public interest and, under presidential order, his remains were returned to the United States for proper burial.

That was in July, 1905, and the last surviving member of the official escort which accompanied the body back to this country is now living in Clearwater, Florida. He is Major Hal Morrison, retired, and now in his nineties. In an interview, he told me the somber story of the hero's journey home.

"I had recently enlisted in the navy and was serving aboard the U.S.S. *Brooklyn* at that time," recalled the major, who switched services later on. "When the *Brooklyn* was dispatched by President Teddy Roosevelt to carry Jones's body back from France, I was tapped for the honor guard."

The *Brooklyn* had docked at the French port of Cherbourg and on July 6, the anniversary of Jones's birth, the hero's remains were escorted up from Paris by both French and American military units.

The flag-draped coffin arrived at the Cherbourg dockside after an impressive ceremony in a Paris church. Every dignitary in the city had attended the service, including the president of France. After the service, the funeral cortege had wound its way through the streets of Paris to the slow roll of muffled drums. As the caisson bearing Jones's coffin passed by, thousands of Parisians lining the funeral route wept openly, as if Jones had been one of their own. It was the greatest tribute ever paid to an American up to that time.

"The heavy metal coffin came aboard the *Brooklyn*

with a full twenty-one-gun salute," explained the major. "It was placed aft, and we stood twenty-four-hour guard over it all across the Atlantic.

"Jones's body was finally brought to Annapolis," said the major. "And that's where it is now, in a special crypt at the Naval Academy."

The magnificent crypt has become a national shrine. But there would have been no hero to place in the tomb had it not been for the efforts of two men—Horace Porter and a far-sighted Frenchman who gave John Paul Jones an honorable burial 113 years before the country he served ever thought of doing so.

"Jones and Barry"   U.S.A., 1937

They Call Her Methuselah

High on a windswept peak in California
lives the world's oldest "mother."

JUBILANT SCIENTISTS AGREED that it was a remarkable
birth. A 4,500-year-old parent had produced forty-
eight tiny living "babies." No one had thought it possible, but the grand old lady they called Methuselah
had confounded her doubters.

Methuselah is the oldest living thing on earth, a
rare bristlecone pine tree that sprouted while the ancient pyramids of Egypt were still young. Growing ten
thousand feet up on an icy, barren mountain top in
the high Sierras, the gnarled old tree has managed to
survive the buffetings of almost five millenniums.

But Methuselah's seeds did not fare so well. The
environment had become just too harsh for them, and

for centuries the little cones have not been able to germinate after falling from the mother tree.

Now, however, things are changing: some of Methuselah's seeds are sprouting once again. The seedlings are not growing under mama's protective branches on the cold mountainside, though. Instead, thanks to some dedicated botanists who recently collected the cones, the "babies" are growing in the greenhouse of the United States Institute of Forest Genetics near Placerville, California.

The Institute—which is in the foothills of the Sierra Nevada—is famous for its study of forest life. It is a research mecca for scientists and conservationists from all over the world, and the news about the little bristlecones has delighted them all. It is still another step forward in man's fight to save what is left of his green and leafy world.

The world of the forest started more than four hundred million years ago, say the scientists. It was then that the first tree appeared—a "naked tree" without bark and very small, not more than two feet high. It was formed of a brand new element in the universe —wood—and it sprang up at the edge of the sea. Without roots, this new form of evolutionary life was sustained through a tangle of tubelike branches which intertwined themselves with moss and seaweed.

Over the ages, the "naked tree" put out leaves and fruits, developed roots, grew tall, and changed into many different forms, all of which reproduced themselves by the countless millions. By the time man appeared, the graceful trees were everywhere and had made for him an earthly paradise.

But man didn't keep his leafy paradise for long. He started sabotaging it early on, and his ravaging hand has written a frightening message on the face of the earth. In North Africa, in Asia, in Greece lie vast areas of powdery dust. Once these regions were covered with dense forests, but centuries of overgrazing and the steady inroads made by fuel gatherers have left them barren of all but scrub vegetation.

Even in ancient times some men worried about the depletion of their woodlands. The Greeks created little "forest preserves" around the many places of worship dedicated to their gods. The Romans set up a loose system of land management by letting out and supervising public forests for private use.

But no one ever did enough, and wherever man settled in numbers, the forests disappeared. Noting this more than two thousand years ago, Plato, the Greek philosopher, lamented the changes which had taken place since his own youth:

> What now remains compared with what then existed is like the skeleton of a sick man, all of the fat and soft earth having wasted away, and only the bare framework of the land being left . . . for there are some mountains which now have nothing but . . . they had trees not very long ago.

But our forests are endangered not only by man's ceaseless use and misuse of them: millions of trees are destroyed each year by man's carelessness as well. These are the ones that go up in smoke. Ninety percent of all forest fires, says the National Forest Service, are caused—or set—by people. Only two percent are started by nature's favorite torch, the lightning bolt.

It was probably lightning that caused the greatest of all forest fires. That was the Peshtigo fire, named after the little Wisconsin farming town where it was first observed.

This was a true holocaust and it burned longer, destroyed more property, and took more lives than any other single fire—forest or otherwise—in history. Only in the blazing cities of war have more souls met flaming death.

The first warning of what was to become a rolling, consuming inferno hit the little town of Peshtigo late on a quiet Sunday afternoon. It was then that someone first smelled wood smoke. But it had been a very dry summer in Wisconsin that year and the people expected some fire in the forest. Although they were worried, they thought it would be just another small blaze, easily beaten back.

But it was not. Quickly, as the people prepared to fight the fire, the volume of smoke increased, grew dense and acrid. Then the sky darkened and with each passing minute the air grew noticeably hotter. The domestic animals began to grow restless, milled around in their pens and pawed the ground. In the streets, the dogs started to howl and run in circles.

Suddenly, a curious sound was borne on the wind. It was, said one survivor later, "like a long line of freight trains approaching." The townspeople, now aware of their danger and thoroughly frightened, gathered in anxious knots and asked each other what they should do to save themselves.

But it was already too late. The sky, which had become almost totally black, now showed a sullen glare over the forest. As the helpless people watched, the glare expanded, grew brighter, redder, more terrible. Then, suddenly, the "freight train" was upon them. In an explosion of thunderous sound, of searing heat and leaping flame, the fire swept out of the forest and over the town.

It took only a few minutes for the great fire storm to do its deadly work before it roared on to wreak further desolation. In the wake of its furious passage, it left not a single building standing and killed 350 of the town's 3,000 inhabitants. Some were burnt in their homes, some overtaken as they fled toward the river. Others died painfully of seared lungs as they stood in the water and breathed the fiery air.

As the fire rolled on, whole towns disappeared, leaving no other trace of their existence but charred ruins and the smell of death.

Not all of those who died, however, perished in the fire. Some, hopelessly trapped in their farmhouses, took a short cut. One man shot all his cattle and then turned the gun on himself. Another killed his entire family and then died by his own terrified hand.

It took six nightmare days for the Peshtigo fire to burn itself out. Sweeping back from Green Bay in a devouring fury, the fire destroyed everything standing in its flaming path. During its savage rampage it incinerated over one million acres of prime land in northeast Wisconsin and part of Michigan. No one has ever been able to calculate how many millions of dollars were lost in buildings, equipment, livestock, crops, and timber.

But the loss of life was known; the fire had killed almost twelve hundred people. That was almost five times the number killed in the Chicago fire.

History has neglected the Peshtigo fire, and the reason for this is not hard to understand. The neglect was caused by the timing of the fire which, by a fantastic coincidence, started on the very same day, and at almost the same hour, as the Chicago fire. That was on October 8, 1871.

When the shocking news—"Chicago is burning!"—flashed out over the wire on that fateful day, it blotted out all other events. The city on the lake was world famous, but who had ever heard of Peshtigo? So it was natural that all attention was focused on Chicago. Everything else was passed over.

And this still holds true. Today, when people speak of great fires, they always name Chicago. Few of them ever mention the greatest, the most "killing" fire of all time, the Peshtigo holocaust.

"Forest Conservation" **U.S.A., 1958**

A Fortune in Blue and Green

If they had only stopped to notice the colors, many poor letter writers would have become rich.

MOST PEOPLE WHO are interested in rare stamps look for mistakes made in design detail—like the famous 24-cent Air Mail Invert, so named because it showed a plane flying upside down. But a few rare stamps are valuable because of their color. And one of these, the Spanish Two Reales Blue, was for a long time branded as a fraud.

Spain issued her first postage stamps on January 1, 1850. They were immediately successful with the people, and soon afterward the government announced that there would be a brand-new stamp issued on January 1, 1851.

The new stamps showed a portrait of Queen Isabella II in an oval frame with the value of each stamp inscribed in letters around the margin. No numbers appeared on the stamp, and each denomination was on a different color paper.

Among the denominations used were the red-tinted Two Reales (at that time Spain's monetary unit) and the blue-tinted Six Reales.

Hundreds of thousands of these stamps, all in perfect order, were turned out, but somewhere during this printing process—for what reason no one can ever know—an error was made when the two-reales plate was briefly used to print on the blue paper of the six-reales stamp. The error was quickly noticed and corrected, but not before some of the flawed stamps escaped into circulation where they were eventually used, lost, and forgotten.

In 1867 a London philatelist found an incorrect Two Reales Blue in a batch of old stamps he had bought from a Spanish dealer. The Englishman promptly wrote an article about his find. But because the flawed stamp had never been noticed before, many collectors branded it as a fraud. The Englishman fought back and soon a lively pro and con argument about the stamp was under way among the world's leading philatelists.

Thirty-two years later, in 1899, in a little shop in Madrid, the validity of the stamp was finally proven. A sheet of the original—and correct—Six-Reales Blues, printed in 1851, was found intact. And the last stamp on the blue sheet, instead of being numbered like its companions, carried the denomination "Two Reales." This should have appeared only on the red sheets.

This discovery, half a century after the stamps were printed, gave absolute proof that the Spanish Two Reales Blue was a rare printing error and not a fraud.

A few of these stamps have turned up since, but their

rarity is reflected in the latest evaluation—$50,000—which was set on one of them.

Another rare stamp with a "colorful" history popped up at the close of the last century.

In 1850 Austria and the German states signed an agreement for the mutual exchange of mail at fixed rates. The separate states (which now make up the German nation) were to issue their own stamps, but the postpaid fee was to be equal for all.

Among the first to agree to this sensible postal arrangement was the little Grand Duchy of Baden, which immediately designed a series of stamps which made their initial appearance on May 1, 1851.

These early Baden stamps were widely used until, replaced by later issues, they finally disappeared altogether. However, if some of the people who used these original stamps had thought to notice their colors instead of just looking at the denominations printed on them, there might have been a few more tidy fortunes in Baden today—because a rare error had occurred in one of the sheets issued in that historic series.

Among several denominations, all with the same design, were the green Six Kreuzer (a monetary unit) and the red Nine Kreuzer. At one point, a careless printer misread the "9" for the "6" (an easy mistake to make when either of the numbers is upside down) and used the "9" plate on the wrong-colored paper. This resulted in a Nine Kreuzer *green* stamp.

As is the case with most stamp errors, this was quickly noticed by alert checkers and the mistake was corrected. Only a handful of the incorrect "Nine Kreuzer Green" managed to get by and into circulation. As the Baden Post Office made no mention of the error, the few misprinted stamps went unnoticed by both public and collectors alike.

Then, in 1894, by an amazing coincidence, three

of these rare stamps came to light. A dealer stumbled on one of them. The other two belonged to a famous collector, Baron Von Turckheim, who had kept his family's vast correspondence for years and found the stamps on some old envelopes. Up until that time the existence of these rare stamps had been unknown even among philatelists.

Although more than one of these stamps exist, their individual value—$45,000—still remains high among collectors.

"Two-Reales Blue"   *Spain, 1851*

Saint Patrick's Purgatory

The most rugged pilgrimage of faith honors an uncanonized saint.

SAINT PATRICK IS the most beloved of all saints. And not only in Ireland. Wherever the lively sons and daughters of Eire are found—from the sidewalks of New York to the outback of Australia—they invoke the name of their most revered saint. With pride and affection, it trips quickly from every Irish tongue. And in his honor, all around the world, are named countless churches, schools, societies, landmarks, and children, sons and daughters alike.

Yet Saint Patrick is not a saint; he has never been canonized by the Church. He is Ireland's holy patron only by reason of tradition and the power of popular acclaim. The love of the Irish people, both Catholic and Protestant, has exalted him to sainthood.

Patrick wasn't Irish either. He was born at the end of the fourth century in west Britain, probably about 385 A.D. His parents were well-to-do Christians who then lived under Roman rule.

At the age of sixteen, young Patrick was captured by sea raiders who carried him off to Ireland and sold him as a slave to a petty king in county Antrim. It was there that the lonely boy, while herding his master's pigs in the wild northern hills, grew deeply religious.

Finally, after six long years, Patrick escaped his bondage and fled to France where he studied for the priesthood. It was during this period that he experienced "visions" and heard "the voice of the Irish people" call him to return and convert them from paganism to the "true faith."

Ordained and made a bishop, Patrick returned to Ireland in 432 and thus began what might be called the greatest apostolic mission in the history of the Church: a dedicated man of boundless belief and enduring strength, Saint Patrick is credited, almost alone, with the conversion of all Ireland.

No one can now tell just how many thousands of pagans Saint Patrick brought to the baptismal font during his missionary life of almost thirty years. What is known, however, is that this astonishing man founded seven hundred churches, ordained more than five thousand priests and consecrated almost four hundred bishops. (There were so many bishops because each of the small and scattered tribes required such a man of authority to guide it.)

At the time of his death in Saul, in 461, Saint Patrick was able to depart in peace knowing that he had firmly established a native church in Ireland.

The Patrician spirit pervades all Ireland and there is not a town or hamlet without some reference to the national apostle. Even the great Protestant cathedral in Dublin is named after him.

But the most ardent expressions of veneration for the Irish saint are found in the pilgrimages taken in his honor. They are all difficult, but the most rugged is the one known as Saint Patrick's Purgatory.

This takes place at lonely Lough Derg (Red Lake) in Donegal, where Saint Patrick first saw his vision of Purgatory. Station Island, in the center of the lake, has been the heart of the pilgrimage for almost fifteen centuries.

Only the most devout worshippers undertake the rigors of Saint Patrick's Purgatory. The pilgrimage is so severe that Pope Pius IX described it as "the last virile example of the ancient canonical penances of the Church." (In 1961, on the fifteen-hundredth anniversary of the saint's death, Vatican City issued a commemorative stamp showing Lough Derg.)

I learned firsthand about this pilgrimage as I sat talking one night in Dublin to a friend, Sheilah Walsh, a columnist on the *Free Press*.

"The pilgrimage takes three days," explained Sheilah. "During that time the only food allowed is a single piece of brown bread and a cup of tea each day. Also, you must remain awake for the first twenty-four hours. And for all three days you must go barefoot, moving constantly in your devotions around the Basilica, the Stations of the Cross, and the rocky beds of the penitent monks, dead now a thousand years." When the exhausted penitents finally sleep, they do so on pallets laid in cold monastic cells. "But when you have finished this pilgrimage there is a wondrous feeling," Sheilah added, "a kind of reborning of your spirit and of your body, as well."

Croagh Patrick, a solitary mountain rising 2,500 steep feet above beautiful Clew Bay, is also the scene of a strenuous pilgrimage. Once a year, on Garland Sunday, the last in July, the devout climb to the summit of Croagh Patrick for a sunrise mass. It was there that Patrick once spent the forty days of Lent fasting and praying for the souls of his Irish "children."

The ascent to the summit of Croagh Patrick (also called The Reek) is made at night and all the pilgrims —sometimes fifty thousand strong—carry lights. They follow a narrow, winding path and, as they move upward on the holy mountain, it is a beautiful sight to see the long thread of their lights weaving slowly through the darkness.

The means for venerating the beloved old saint do not all spring from the past. The twentieth century has made its own contribution to keeping Patrick's memory green.

In June of every year, all the international jet planes of Aer Lingus—the Irish airlines—are temporarily taken out of service and lined up together on the tarmac of Dublin's Shannon Airport.

There, in the only ceremony of its kind in the world and before an altar built just for the occasion, a priest blesses all the planes and commends them, their passengers, and their crews into the hands of God.

Foremost among these giant jets, of course, is the one named Saint Patrick.

"Saint Patrick"   *Ireland, 1961*

He Outlived His Great-Grandsons

He was born the year George Washington was inaugurated President.

THE OLDEST MAN ever known to have lived was a Zenu Indian from Colombia, South America. He stood four feet four inches in his unstockinged feet, had outlived five wives and all his children and grandchildren. He was born the year George Washington became president of the United States—in 1789.

His name was Javier Pereira and I met him in his native Colombia when he was 166 years old. He was then living in the town of Montería as a ward of the church.

Javier's great age was first attested to by the authorities of Montería, who knew his history. They had several written records concerning his longevity, along with abundant evidence in the form of statements by other very ancient Zenu Indians. They said that when they were small children they had known Javier as a very old chief already renowned for his long life. And, according to tribal history, their grandfathers before them had known Javier.

The best evidence of his great age came from Javier himself. Questioned at length by historians and anthropologists concerning events which had occurred in the early 1800's, the old Indian came up with such long and detailed accounts of those times that the scientists went away convinced that he had lived that far back. Javier was unable to read or write, so only firsthand experience could account for his knowledge of events that had taken place over a century before. He had to have been there in order to know about them.

Of particular interest to historians was Javier's account of the siege of Cartagena in 1815 and the famine which followed it. He described these graphically, also telling of a wound he'd received as a teen-aged soldier during a Spanish attack.

I was fascinated by Javier and made arrangements to fly him to New York for medical study. Before doing so, I had him brought to the hospital of San Vicente de Paul in Medellín, Colombia, for tests of his age. Specialists in geriatric medicine there said that he was well into his second century, but they could not tell just how far. They also said that his health was excellent and that he could travel.

Javier made his entry into the United States by way of Miami, where we stayed overnight. The next morning, at the airport, newsmen, television crews, and the curious swarmed about Javier as we boarded a plane for the north.

The little Indian, alert and watchful, took all the commotion in stride. Then suddenly, as he continued to observe the surging mass of bobbing, weaving, shouting, lens-clicking people around him, he turned to the interpreter who had accompanied him from Colombia and said: "Let's go. They are all crazy." It was a comment we were to hear often from Javier during the weeks that followed.

At the airport in New York, the crowd scene was repeated—with the volume turned up. More newsmen and camera crews came out to see the ancient little man than had ever come out to cover the arrival of that show-stopper, Marilyn Monroe. The resulting stories and pictures made headlines throughout the world the next day.

From the airport, Javier went directly to New York Hospital–Cornell Medical Center, in mid-Manhattan. He stayed at the hospital for ten days and underwent every test, physical and psychological, that was known to medicine.

Although the doctors made it clear that there was no scientific method to pinpoint his exact age, they did find that Javier was a very, very old man and said that nonmedical evidence indicated that he was "more than 150 years old."

However, what most astonished the doctors was the superb physical condition of this centenarian plus. It was found that Javier's heart action, arteries, and blood pressure were those of a healthy twenty-year-old man. Although his hearing and his sight were slightly impaired, he was mentally "alert and observing," his memory was "excellent," and his brain showed "no sign of deterioration." His blood cholesterol was not much above one hundred milligrams, which is far below the average for a normal adult.

Although Javier had some arthritis in his hands and his skin showed very advanced age, the hospital reported that "his bones and joints were in a condition that many a young man might envy."

What made Javier live so long, and in such good health?

Well, surmised the doctors, he lived a natural life quite free of stress, his diet was a simple one of rice, vegetables, and fruits, and he probably came from a tribe of unusually long-lived people. Contrary to most health rules, however, Javier liked to smoke and he also drank great quantities of coffee, one of Colombia's major products.

Shortly after he left the hospital, Javier Pereira returned to his quiet life in Montería. He died there a few years later, still spinning tales of his wonderful trip to a mighty city far in the north. Like his arrival at the New York airport, his death also made headlines throughout the world.

Javier was not a philosophical man, but he did have his own recipe for a long life. It would not rate a gold star from the medical profession, but the ancient little Indian felt it had served him well. If it had not helped to increase his years, it had certainly made them happier.

He said: "Don't worry, drink lots of coffee, and smoke a good cigar."

"*Javier Pereira*"   Colombia, 1956

The Luckless Spaniard

He stood alone on a mountaintop and became the first European to look west across the Pacific Ocean.

VASCO NÚÑEZ DE Balboa was a magnificent failure. Nothing he ever did worked out for him, and his greatest achievement—the discovery of the Pacific Ocean—eventually led to his death.

Born in Spain in 1475, Balboa grew to manhood during the early days of the "Golden Age of Exploration." At the age of twenty-five he sailed for the New World, not as a captain but a mere crewman.

Reaching the West Indies, he soon abandoned the sea and settled down as a planter on the island of Hispaniola (which today shares the nations of Haiti and the Dominican Republic). But he fared poorly there. Within a few years he was destitute, and his creditors were closing in. Out of desperation, Balboa grabbed his sword and a suit of clothes and stowed away on a ship bound for Central America.

But he was as bad a stowaway as he was a planter, and he was discovered soon after the ship got under way. The leader of the expedition, Martín de Enciso, was furious with the stowaway at first. However, as Balboa proved a worthy seaman, he kept him on.

When the expedition learned that the original site of the colony on the Gulf of Darien (near Panama) had been wiped out by Indians, Enciso took Balboa's advice and founded a new settlement on the other side of the Gulf, where the Indians were said to be friendlier.

Santa María de la Antigua, as the new colony was called, prospered for a while. But rivalries arose. Enciso was deported and Balboa replaced him as the colony's leader.

For the first time in his life, things seemed to be going Balboa's way. He made friends with the Indians and gathered gold from the area without incident. But it was too good to last. When he sent to Spain for confirmation of his new post, he was ordered to "do something important" or be recalled to Madrid to account for his actions . . . and that would mean prison.

Balboa explained his plight to his adopted blood brother, Comaco, the local native chieftain. The Indian told him there was a sea beyond the mountains and another country where gold was plentiful.

That was enough for the desperate Spaniard. Gathering a force of sixty-six men, he set out on his now famous march of discovery.

For twenty-five days, Balboa's expedition hacked its way through jungles so dense the sun was blotted from sight. Then one morning, after crossing the Cordillera de San Blas mountains, on what is now the Isthmus of Panama, the smell of salt reached the exhausted explorers. Leaving his men at the foot of the hill, Balboa climbed to its crest and stood alone in awe of what he saw—the wide blue-green expanse of an unknown sea, what we today know as the Pacific Ocean.

He called it Mar del Sur, the South Sea, and later in the day waded into the salty water to take possession of this sea—and all the lands it touched—in the name of the rulers of Castile. The year was 1513.

The discovery should have ended Balboa's troubles. Instead, it only served to complicate them.

There was still the land of gold the Indians had told him about. He must find it. But while he was planning to build a fleet to seek the land of fortune, other adventurers set out for his colony. Among them was Pedro Arias de Avila, more commonly known as Pedrarias Dávila.

The two men had different opinions on how to run a colony. Balboa believed in befriending the Indians. Dávila preferred to conquer them. The argument grew into a power struggle. Dávila, with fifteen hundred armed men to back him up, finally had Balboa arrested.

Falsely charged with treason and murder, the forty-two-year-old explorer was convicted and beheaded along with four compatriots in the public square of the colony he had helped to found, Santa María de la Antigua.

Only four years earlier he had first set eyes on the Pacific. He had found an ocean . . . but he had never been able to find luck.

"Balboa" U.S.A., 1913

Every Mother Is Unique

It is the first word formed in infancy—and often the last spoken at death.

IN EGYPT'S VALLEY of the Kings, where ancient pharaohs sleep beneath their vast monuments, there is the tomb of a queen which bears this inscription:

One thing alone is better and more beautiful than anything else beneath the rays of the great Sun God. It is a mother.

This is the earliest known memorial to mention the word mother, and it shows clearly that mankind has honored motherhood for a very long time.

Public veneration of motherhood in this country started in 1908 with the celebration of the first Mother's

Day. It was initiated by Anna Jarvis, a young Philadelphia woman who, mourning the loss of her own beloved mother, suggested that a day should be set aside in honor of all mothers, living and dead. She chose the second Sunday in May because it was the anniversary of her own mother's death.

The idea caught on so quickly and gained such immediate acceptance that only six years later, in 1914, Congress passed an act setting aside the second Sunday in May in honor of mothers.

While the observance was brand new in America, our English cousins have had a special day devoted to mothers since medieval times. They call it Mothering Sunday, and it falls on the fourth Sunday of Lent. On this day, the English visit their mothers, bringing candy, flowers, and "simnels," little spiced cakes baked for the occasion.

The custom did not cross the Atlantic with the early Puritan settlers because these stern folk disapproved of all holidays and particularly rejected Mothering Sunday. This holiday, they knew, stemmed from Asia Minor where, long before Christ, the early pagans had a day for honoring Cybele, "Mother of the Gods."

The Romans adopted the festival as the Feast of Hilaria and, after Christianity took root in Rome, it became Mother Church Day, celebrated on the fourth Sunday of Lent. Then it was transplanted to England and modified.

So, with its Roman Catholic—as well as pagan—overtones it is easy to see why Mothering Sunday was left back in England by the rigid, frosty Puritans when they set sail for the New World.

Mother is one of the most frequently used words in all languages. It is usually the first word formed in infancy and is often the last word spoken by men—

but rarely by women—before death silences speech forever.

Even John Wilkes Booth had last words for his shocked and suffering parent as he lay dying of a bullet wound after his capture by Federal troops. "Tell my mother I died for my country," he gasped. "I thought I did it for the best. Useless! Useless!"

Famous men often sing the praises of their mothers. Lincoln, speaking of Nancy Hanks, said: "All that I am, or hope to be, I owe to my angel mother."

Napoleon esteemed his mother, Laetitia Buonaparte, above all women. "Mother of Kings" was the title bestowed on her when her conquering son set his brothers and a sister on the thrones of vanquished nations.

Laetitia lived to see all her children dishonored or dead. She ended her days alone in Rome, deriving her only comfort from endlessly rereading a letter written by Napoleon before his death in exile on the island of St. Helena. It concluded with the words: "My mother is unique among women."

All mothers, of course, are unique, but occasionally one is so extraordinary that she confounds the world.

Such was the case in May, 1939, when Lena Medina gave birth to a fine baby boy in the maternity hospital of Lima, Peru. Lena Medina created a chapter in medical history by being an astonishing five years of age at the time—the youngest human ever known to bear a child. She and her son are healthy, attractive, and above average in intelligence, and still live in Paris.

The oldest mother, according to a record in Paris, was Paule Fieshi. Paule gave birth to a living infant, a boy, on December 1, 1742. Her age was officially witnessed by the doctor as ninety.

The busiest mother ever known was undoubtedly Barbara Schmotzer, a German woman who lived in the town of Bonningheim. She mothered fifty-three children, fifteen girls and thirty-eight boys. They were the combined offspring of herself and her husband, plus the lively fruits of his previous marriage. Several multiple births also helped raise the family membership to this astonishing figure. Busy Barbara went to her deserved rest in 1504, but she was not forgotten. In 1934 her home town erected a plaque to her memory and dubbed her the most motherly of mothers.

Mother Goose is certainly the best known mother among the small fry. And she really did live. She was the mother of the great Frankish king Charlemagne. Her deep compassion for the hordes of poor children of her medieval time made her the generous and tender patron of thousands of suffering waifs. But she was a big and awkward woman and was given the unhappy nickname of "Queen Goosefoot." From this grew the legend of Mother Goose.

The most informed mother (about the doings of her child) was without question the parent of Richard Haldane, the famous lord chancellor of England who died in 1928. "I wrote to my mother every single day from 1877 to her death in 1925," notes Lord Haldane in his memoirs, thereby achieving the half-century record for devotion in the filial correspondence department.

The most tragic mother must certainly have been Queen Anne, who came to the throne of England in 1702. Poor Anne gave birth to seventeen sons and daughters, but not a single child survived her. Only one boy, the little Duke of Gloucester, even reached the age of eleven. The royal mother died heartbroken and alone in 1714.

Perhaps the most faithful mother was a London woman who lived late in the last century. A poor widow, she had one son who ran away from home at the age of fourteen. She had no idea where he was, but because he had been partial to hot cross buns, she baked a batch of them every Good Friday. Then she sat down in the kitchen to wait for her son to come and eat them. She never saw him again, but this faithful mother kept her curious vigil for more than forty years, until she died.

It was, of course, the sort of thing that only mothers do.

"Whistler's Mother"   *U.S.A., 1934*

The Day the Island
Blew Its Top

The thunder of its explosion was heard three thousand miles away.

THERE ARE MANY active volcanoes in Indonesia, in the South Pacific. And that is where the world's greatest explosion oc　　　' on August 26, 1883. That was the day nature gave a mighty heave, belched up killing gases in multimegaton force, and sent the island of Krakatoa sky high.

Krakatoa was—and the stump of what's left of it still is—a volcanic island in the Sunda Strait, near Sumatra. It is part of the Indonesian chain, and the historic eruption of the volcano was the greatest single explosion of any volcano the world has ever known. No eruption of those notorious Italian killers, Etna and Vesuvius, nor of Mount Pelée in this hemisphere, has ever come close to equaling Krakatoa's destructiveness.

For some time before the explosion, Krakatoa had given warning of what was to come. From deep within the volcano had been heard ominous rumblings and mutterings. From its head, rising almost three thousand feet above lush green slopes, had come bilious puffs of dense smoke.

But the islanders paid no attention to the volcano's signals of distress. They were used to the sleeping giant and its intermittent growling. Familiarity bred its usual indifference to danger, and few fled the island for havens of safety elsewhere despite the warnings.

Even flight could not have saved many of the doomed islanders. They could not have fled far enough nor fast enough to escape the deadly magnitude of Krakatoa's eruption when it finally came.

With the first violent upheaval of the volcano, most of the island disappeared at once. In the turbulent process, a thousand-foot-deep hole was gouged out of the ocean floor and the sea rushed in, hissing beneath the fiery rain of ash from above. In this monstrous convulsion of nature, more than 35,000 souls were known to have perished—all asphyxiated, crushed, burned, buried alive, or drowned by the inrushing water from the surrounding sea.

The eruption of Krakatoa continued unabated for two days. During that time it changed forever the entire shape of the Sunda Strait, created islands where none had existed before, and hurled debris clear across the Indian Ocean to Madagascar.

Around the island as it rolled and heaved in its death throes, the steaming sea raged for days. Churned up finally was a vast tidal wave that rushed out over the Pacific to swamp hundreds of ships, flood smaller islands, and ravage shorelines as far away as seven thousand miles. It even pushed at the rocky base of Gibraltar in the distant Mediterranean.

The thundering noise made by the incredible explosion was heard in cities three thousand miles distant. And out of Krakatoa's blasting interior rose a fiery column of molten lava and ash, its density estimated at four cubic miles and its height at seventeen miles straight up. Carried high above the earth by global winds, ash from Krakatoa fell on cities as far away and as widely separated as London, Lima, and Cape Town. The fine pumice left over from the eruption stayed in the atmosphere for years and, by its presence, changed the colors of sunsets everywhere before it settled down to earth again.

No other natural disaster has ever had such far-reaching effects as the explosion of Krakatoa.

This was again made evident in 1956 by a party of geologists attached to the American Corps of Engineers who were deep-drilling in icy Greenland. Working through an area of permafrost, they extracted a sample core in which they found an identifiable layer of dust from Krakatoa.

This dust from the world's greatest explosion had not only been borne on upper air currents from one hemisphere to another, it had also drifted from below the equator on one side of the world all the way up to the Arctic circle on the other—a distance of more than twenty thousand miles.

What little now remains of Krakatoa still stirs with volcanic activity on occasion. As late as 1927 it erupted again in an explosion forceful enough to form another, smaller island nearby. This little island, taking its cue perhaps from its violent mother, also erupted a few years later. By a curious twist of nature, it neatly deposited enough debris in the deep hole made by the 1883 eruption to form still a third little island.

"Erupting Volcano"   Indonesia, 1954

He Gave Us Our National "Attic"

It took a ten-year battle before John Quincy Adams could accept one of the strangest inheritances this country has ever received.

FOR THE INCREASE AND DIFFUSION OF KNOWLEDGE AMONG MEN

1846 · SMITHSONIAN INSTITUTION · 1946
3¢ UNITED STATES POSTAGE

THEY CALL IT "the nation's attic" and many people shake their heads in disbelief at the architecture of the turreted red-sandstone "castle" that stands beside the Mall in Washington, D.C.

But the story of that Smithsonian Institution and the manner in which it was established are far stranger than either its nickname or the seemingly out-of-place appearance that it offers to the millions of people who visit it annually.

To begin with, the Institution was established with funds left to this nation by the illegitimate son of a British nobleman. And it became what he envisioned only through the persistent efforts of a far-sighted man who had once been president of the United States.

James Smithson was born in 1765, the son of Sir Hugh Smithson, first Duke of Northumberland, and Elizabeth Macie, who was a direct descendant of King Henry VII.

The young Englishman used his unmarried's mother's name during the early years of his life. So it was as James Macie that he attained his master's degree from Oxford at the age of twenty-one.

Less than a year later the brilliant young scholar was elected to membership in the Royal Society, possibly the youngest man ever to be so honored by that renowned British organization. In the years that followed, he became one of England's most respected experimental chemists.

Despite his many accomplishments, the extent of his success in England was limited by the fact of his illegitimate birth. To escape this shadow, James Macie, after the death of his mother, changed his name to Smithson—after his natural father—and moved to France. There he continued to work at his scientific experiments.

Smithson was highly successful in his work on the Continent, but eventually he ran into political trouble. He was bitterly opposed to Napoleon and publicly protested the Corsican's rise to power in France. For this he was arrested and not even a clemency plea by the king of Denmark was able to save him from jail.

Freed several years later, Smithson moved his base of operations to Genoa, Italy. He continued to work at several projects, but his long prison term had drained away much of his physical strength and he died in 1829, at the age of sixty-four.

Shortly after he was buried in Genoa's British cemetery, the terms of Smithson's strange will became known. His entire estate of more than a half million dollars was bequeathed to his nephew, Henry James Hungerford.

However, in the event Hungerford died without children of his own, the money was to go to the United States of America, to found in Washington, under the name of the Smithsonian Institution, an "establishment for the increase and diffusion of knowledge amongst men."

Hungerford died six years later without heirs, thus setting the stage for the strange aftermath to his uncle's will.

News of the inheritance reached President Andrew Jackson in 1836, and he turned to Congress for advice. What, he asked, should he do about this unusual matter? Congress was as much puzzled by the bequest as the president. So a committee was formed to decide if Smithson's handsome gift was acceptable and, if so, how the money could be used to conform with the terms of his will.

The chairman of the committee was John Quincy Adams, once president himself. His study proved, at least to his satisfaction, that not only was the inheritance acceptable, but that it could provide this young country with a much-needed scientific institution.

Congress agreed with the first conclusion, but not all its members agreed with the second. So Adams found himself embroiled in a fight that went on for ten full years before he finally got Congress to erect a simple building to house a museum of scientific materials, a chemical laboratory, a library, an art gallery, and lecture facilities.

Only income from the bequest was to be used. The principal would be held by the Treasury Department and administered by a board of regents.

Thus the Smithsonian Institution was born on August 10, 1846.

In 1903, long after the Institution had proved its value, Gilbert H. Grosvenor, first editor of the *National*

Geographic magazine, succeeded in convincing the nation and the regents of the Institution that Smithson's remains should be moved to this country from his grave in Italy. In January of the following year, seventy-five years after his death, the bones of the man whose fortune made possible the establishment of the renowned Smithsonian arrived in Washington, D.C. Today all that is left of James Smithson rests in a marble tomb just inside the Institution's main entrance.

Over the years other buildings have been added to the original one, and the vast Smithsonian now serves as one of the nation's great cultural and scientific centers—an enduring American monument to the fortune and memory of an illegitimate Englishman who never even set foot in the United States:

"The Smithsonian Institution" U.S.A., 1946

El Cid

A hero to friend and foe, he fought against both.

ONE OF THE medieval world's most fabled heroes was a handsome, full-bearded, daring Spaniard named Rodrigo Díaz de Bivar.

Although his amazing life has been the subject of countless ballads and folk tales, few have known his real name. Throughout the ages, he has been known simply as El Cid.

But under either name, this hero's tale is one of the strangest in all of history.

Díaz is believed to have been born in 1040 in Burgos, one of the major cities in the province of Castile. He was the son of a Spanish nobleman and brought up in the court of the king of Castile.

At a very early age he proved to be such a brave and brilliant soldier that he was made chief general of the royal army by Sancho, the reigning king.

In those days the Moors ruled large portions of Spain, and war with them was an almost constant fact of life. But under the young general's leadership, the Castilians began to score a number of major victories over their persistent enemies.

However, at the Battle of Zamaora, in 1072, King Sancho was killed—some say murdered by his brother's sympathizers—and his younger brother, Alfonso, succeeded to the throne.

The intrigue and mystery which surrounded Sancho's death sharply divided the Castilian army and many of the nobles waited impatiently to see the direction General Díaz would take before declaring their allegiance to the new king.

But the hero general was a Castilian first, and he quickly lined up in support of Alfonso, bringing most of the disgruntled royalty with him.

Peace within the army was not to last, however. Alfonso was jealous of anyone who had enjoyed his brother's favor and, despite Díaz's great service to the crown, the new king soon found reason—sufficient to satisfy himself, at least—to send the great soldier into exile.

Determined to fight on, Díaz became a soldier of fortune. Gathering a substantial army of his own about him, he hired out to anyone who would foot the costs of that army.

The Moors, the ancient enemy that he had opposed on behalf of Castile, were quick to recognize his value and enlisted his new army in their ranks.

As had been the case in the past, his courage and military genius quickly won him a place in the affections of his former enemies. So impressed were his

Moorish comrades that they dubbed him El Cid, which means "the lord" in Arabic.

Eventually in his new role he conquered the Spanish province of Valencia, and with his wife (ironically, a niece of King Alfonso) established himself as ruler of that sector of his native land.

Before his death in 1099, El Cid once more altered his loyalty and returned to the wars under the banner of Spain, again taking to the field in opposition to the Moors.

Thus the Spanish national hero whose exploits often have been likened to those of England's King Arthur proved once again his love for his native country.

In recognition of his contributions to Spanish history, in 1921 Alfonso XIII, a descendant of the man who had exiled the great warrior nearly nine centuries earlier, presided at a theatrical patriotic ceremony which transferred the remains of this great man to a grandiose tomb in the cathedral at Burgos, his birthplace.

But the strangest fact of all is that this greatest of Spanish heroes continues to be known by the name El Cid—an honor bestowed on him by Spain's most determined enemies, the Moors.

"El Cid"   Spain, 1949

A Stamp Put the Canal Through Panama

Without a Frenchman's guile, the Big Ditch would have been dug elsewhere.

HAD IT NOT been for a clever Frenchmen and a telltale stamp, the Panama Canal would not exist today. Instead, the great waterway would now flow through Nicaragua.

The mastermind behind the Panama plan was a brilliant young French engineer named Philippe Jean Bunau-Varilla. The strange story of Bunau-Varilla, Panama, and the now bitterly contested canal started in the closing years of the last century.

International trade was booming then and everyone agreed that a canal linking the Atlantic and Pacific oceans was needed to speed up commerce between East and West. A waterway through Central America would chop off eight thousand miles of sailing around Cape Horn.

The first to act on the canal were the French. In 1878 a company headed by Ferdinand de Lesseps, builder of the Suez Canal, signed a limited-time contract with Colombia to build a waterway across the Isthmus of Panama, then a part of Colombian territory. Digging operations on the canal began the following year, but de Lesseps was not to repeat his Suez success in Panama. Bedeviled by increasing problems, the canal venture came to a halt. The French abandoned it less than a decade after they began, leaving behind shattered hopes, tons of rusting equipment, and a partly dug waterway.

They also left behind Bunau-Varilla, a bold and brilliant young Frenchman who, at the age of only twenty-six, had been made chief engineer of the defunct canal company. Bunau-Varilla had dreamed of a canal across the isthmus since his earliest boyhood, when he first read of the Suez. Now he refused to give up his dream. If the French couldn't build the canal, then the Americans would.

The young engineer took himself to Washington. There he bombarded everyone, from the president on down, with his impassioned arguments for completing the Panama Canal. At his own expense he roamed the United States, giving lectures to plead his cause.

But Americans were not too interested in his project. True, the United States had decided to build a canal. But the favored route was across Nicaragua, the little Central American country just to the north of the isthmus. This route would be longer, but it would be easier to build and cheaper to maintain. It would not require the costly and complex series of locks needed to carry ships across the rugged Isthmus of Panama.

In the spring of 1902, when Congress met to hear final arguments on which route the American-built canal would take, it was widely acknowledged that the Nicaraguan site would be endorsed. The Panama plan had few supporters in Congress.

Then one of history's dramatic ironies took place. Just a few days before Congress was to vote on the canal, a volcano erupted in the Caribbean and started sympathetic rumblings in surrounding volcanic areas.

This underground activity aroused panic in Nicaragua, which badly needed the revenue the canal would bring. The country's volcanic mountains had once been advanced as an argument against building a canal there, but the Nicaraguans had succeeded in assuring U.S. officials that all her volcanoes were extinct. Now the Nicaraguans hurriedly issued another statement saying again that there was absolutely no volcanic activity within the country's borders.

But Nicaragua failed to reckon with the resourceful Bunau-Varilla. The energetic engineer remembered that just a few years earlier Nicaragua had issued a stamp bearing a picture of Momotombo. This was one of the country's most famous volcanic mountains and it loomed over the route of the proposed American canal. Momotombo was said to be extinct—yet the stamp showed its peak crowned with a tall plume of smoke, as befits an active volcano.

Scurrying around Washington, Bunau-Varilla managed to track down ninety of these Nicaraguan stamps, one for each of the senators who was about to vote on the canal route. The following morning on each senatorial desk there was an envelope containing a stamp and a note in Bunau-Varilla's handwriting: "Official witness to volcanic activity in Nicaragua."

The senators studied the stamp, did some hard thinking, and then reversed themselves. When the vote was taken a few days later, the Senate decided to pick up the unexpired French contract and build the canal across Panama instead of Nicaragua.

Now a new threat arose. Colombia was having second thoughts about the canal. Other countries besides the United States were interested in building a passage across the isthmus. It would be to the advantage of Colombia to stall for time, let the old French contract expire, and then negotiate a new one on better terms.

But Bunau-Varilla was not to be denied his victory. If Colombia stood in the way, then she must be bypassed. So Panama had a bloodless revolution which freed it from Colombia. The liberation leader was Manuel Amador, a Panamanian political hero. But the principal schemer behind the revolt was Bunau-Varilla.

Of the revolution, Bunau-Varilla said later: "To realize the Panama Canal . . . I was constrained to make myself responsible for a new independent state in South America."

Bunau-Varilla was the heart of the infant Republic of Panama. He organized the new government, financed it out of his own pocket, drew up its constitution, created a code of laws for its courts. He even designed the first Republic of Panama flag. His wife bought the silk at Macy's department store in New York and sewed it together at the old Waldorf Astoria hotel.

Finally, Bunau-Varilla secured worldwide recognition of Panama's independence and then made himself first Panamanian minister to the United States.

As minister, Bunau-Varilla drew up the famous treaty which gave to our government the right to own and operate a canal through Panama "in perpetuity." This treaty, which bears his name and is still in force (and the subject of the present heated controversy), was written by Bunau-Varilla in just a few hours, "between breakfast and lunch," as he recalled later. It was signed on November 18, 1903.

Only once did this extraordinary man ever tell his story to the American people. That was in February, 1940. He was past eighty and living in Paris, when I arranged to have him interviewed over the CBS network by short wave. The interview took place in a Paris studio and the interviewer was a young news commentator named Eric Sevareid.

The great old man was delighted to be heard at last and was at pains to clear the United States of any association with the revolution. It was then that he said:

"President Theodore Roosevelt had no participation whatever in the creation of the new Republic of Panama. No American had any part in either the conception or realization of my project to change the sovereignty of the state."

A few months later, Philippe Bunau-Varilla, true father of Panama and the great canal, was dead.

"Mount Momotomba"   Nicaragua, 1900

"Place It on Top of the Hill"

Men in the foxholes cheered and whistled as the flag became visible through the smoke of battle.

NO COMBAT PHOTO has ever had greater impact than the one of a half-dozen helmeted marines raising the stars and stripes on Iwo Jima's Mount Suribachi during World War II. It was published in hundreds of newspapers and magazines, won a Pulitzer prize for the photographer Joe Rosenthal, was glorified in song, and became the model for the Marine Corps Memorial in Arlington, Virginia.

Secretary of the Navy James V. Forrestal witnessed the event from a landing craft headed toward the beach and told General "Howling Mad" Smith, "Holland, the raising of that flag on Suribachi means a marine corps for the next five hundred years.'"

Yet the famed picture is not a true representation of the event it depicts.

Without detracting one iota from either the heroic event or the photographer, the scene as it appeared in the Rosenthal picture actually was "staged" some time after the original raising took place.

This is how it happened.

About midway through 1944, at the urging of a number of army air force generals, the joint chiefs of staff decided to add Iwo Jima to the list of islands to be invaded on the road to Japan.

The reasons were twofold—to provide an emergency strip for crippled B-29 Superfortresses already engaged in bombing the enemy homeland, and to use as a strip for shorter-range fighters to escort the bombers on those missions.

Iwo was a tiny spot of land—no more than five miles long and two-and-a-half wide—about halfway between Saipan, the home of the B-29s, and Tokyo. Its most prominent landmark was a 556-foot hill at its south end, dubbed Mount Suribachi.

On February 19, 1945, after nearly six weeks of concentrated aerial bombardment and thousands of rounds of warship fire, the marines of the Fourth and Fifth Divisions stormed ashore.

From the very beginning there was fanatical resistance from the more than 21,000 Japanese defenders who had gone underground during those attacks. Virtually every foot of ground wrested from them was paid for at an awesome price in blood. Later, marines would describe the attack as a "nightmare in hell."

However, despite everything, yard by yard the determined marines literally tore the island from the enemy's grasp.

By the third day ashore, February 21, they had surrounded Mount Suribachi and begun preparations for the final assault on its important heights. However, it was not until the morning of February 23 that the first of the attackers neared the pinnacle.

Then with the goal in sight, Lt. Col. Chandler Johnson, who had brought an American flag ashore with him, sent the banner to 1st Lt. Harold Schrier, leader of the men near the summit, with instructions to place it "on top of the hill."

At the lip of the crater which topped Suribachi, Schrier and his men were pinned down by a last-second burst of fire. During that pause one of the men discovered a long piece of pipe and tied the fifty-four-by-twenty-eight-inch flag to one end of it.

Then, at 10:20, the lieutenant and five of his men rushed to the hill's peak and raised the flag while a photographer from *Leatherneck* magazine took pictures. He was the only one present at that crucial moment.

Just as the banner fluttered in the breeze, two hidden Japanese popped out from a nearby cave. One hurled a grenade at the photographer; the other was shot down as the exposed marines leaped for the crater's safety. The photographer, tumbling down the side of the hole more than fifty feet to the bottom, smashed his camera in the process.

Meanwhile, from below, the small flag was barely visible—but those who were able to see it cheered mightily, and from the ships offshore horns and whistles screeched in salute.

Colonel Johnson, who had sent the original flag up the hill, raced to a landing craft that was just nosing into shore and grabbed a much larger flag from its crew. Then, turning to his adjutant, he insisted it be sent to replace the original.

Enter now Joe Rosenthal, a veteran Associated Press photographer.

Sensing the opportunity, he followed the runner who

carried the replacement banner and scrambled his way up the mountain. Once at the top he positioned himself astride a pile of nearby stones and when the larger flag was raised, at about noon, Rosenthal snapped his now famous picture.

Another month passed before the island was secured. More than 4,500 marines and nearly 500 sailors gave their lives. Considering the length of the battle, it proved to be the greatest toll of World War II.

Of the 21,000 enemy defenders, fewer than 3,000 survived. Among the casualties was their commander, Lt. Gen. Tadamichi Kuribayashi. He committed hara-kiri on March 27, when it was evident the island had been lost.

Thus the familiar flag raising, the symbol that has come to signify the glory of the United States Marines, took place weeks before the tiny island of Iwo Jima was actually in American hands.

Even more significantly, the original act of raising the flag on Iwo Jima occurred almost two hours before the famous picture was taken.

No matter.

Both flag raisings deserve their place among the great moments of American history.

"Iwo Jima"   U.S.A., 1945

They Changed Medical Practice

Two brothers who gave a new meaning to "teamwork."

NO ONE IN the major medical centers of the world paid the slightest attention to the opening of a new hospital in the small southeastern Minnesota village of Rochester in 1889.

St. Mary's Hospital was just another tiny institution in a relatively obscure corner of the rural upper Midwest. Staffed mainly by a father and his two sons who had only recently graduated from medical schools near their home, the hospital seemed just another minor medical venture.

Today, almost a hundred years after that founding, no one ignores the famous Mayo Clinic which sprang from those humble beginnings, nor the two brothers who revolutionized the practice of medicine.

The theories and procedures that William James and Charles Horace Mayo introduced in their clinic have been the blueprints for hundreds of similar institutions throughout the world. And from these the patient, more than anyone else, has benefited.

Dr. Will, the older of the two Mayo brothers, was born in LeSueur, Minnesota, in 1861 and graduated in medicine from the University of Michigan in 1883. He specialized in gallstone, cancer, and stomach operations.

Dr. Charles was four years younger and born in Rochester, the city in which the brothers would gain worldwide fame. He was educated at Northwestern University, graduating with the class of 1888. He became noted for his success in reducing the death rate in goiter surgery.

But their personal surgical skills, which in themselves can be termed almost legendary, tell only half the story. It was their coordination of the work of one specialist with another that was unique. And that ability to organize the specialized skills of others into efficient health care teams—something which had never been done before—revolutionized medical practice.

Probably no two brothers ever were more dissimilar. William was reserved, imperturbable, decisive, and generally considered the leader. Charles, on the other hand, had the supreme gift of the common touch. Fortunately, the two personalities dovetailed perfectly.

Until early in the twentieth century, the two brothers performed all the surgery at St. Mary's. As their successes increased, however, their reputations grew until it no longer was possible for them to keep abreast of their rapidly growing workload. To take up the slack, they began adding talented young physicians from varying specialized fields of medicine to their staff. To better utilize the specialized skills of these doctors, the Mayos began working them in teams. Out of this grew the

Mayos' coordinated team method for treating patients.

From the outset, their clinic proved a great financial success despite the brothers' policy of charging only as much as each patient could afford. Then, in 1915, to foster even greater efficiency, they established the Mayo Foundation of Medical Education and Research at the graduate school of the University of Minnesota. That move transformed the clinic from a two-man partnership into a voluntary association of physicians and specialists in allied fields. Literally hundreds of similar clinics now exist throughout the world.

During World War I the brothers alternated as chief consultants for all surgical services in the U.S. Army. Both attained the high level of brigadier general in the medical corps reserve.

In 1933 both members of the renowned medical team retired, but the foundation they had built was sound enough to outlast them. Ironically, the two men died only two months apart. Charles, the younger, succumbed in Chicago on May 26, 1939. Two months and two days later, on July 28, 1939, William also passed away.

Today nearly 200,000 patients register annually at the clinic the brothers founded. In its long history it has cared for almost three million people. Moreover, the medical innovations the brothers introduced continue to bring healing and hope to millions more throughout the world.

The contributions of the Mayo brothers to humanity are literally incalculable.

"The Doctors Mayo" U.S.A., 1964

Man of the Wilderness Road

The urge always to wander was deep in the blood of the man who became the nation's greatest frontiersman.

"IF YOU CAN see the smoke from your neighbor's chimney, it's time to move on."

Those words, attributed to Daniel Boone, typify the philosophy of the American frontiersman who has become the symbol of this nation's first move westward.

Boone, in real life, was considerably different from the man who has been portrayed in story, song, and motion pictures. He was, for example, only a scant five feet seven inches tall. And he thoroughly despised the coonskin cap with the bushy tail which most frontiersmen adopted. Instead, he favored—and always wore —a beaver hat.

Few need to be reminded of the facts of Boone's life.

He was born in western Pennsylvania in 1734 and moved to North Carolina while still in his teens. There he grew into a superb hunter and marksman, acquiring skills which were useful when he served under General Braddock in the French and Indians Wars.

Later, learning about the hidden marvels of unexplored Kentucky, Boone pioneered that vast region, blazed its now famous Wilderness Road, and founded its first permanent settlement at Boonesboro.

As a frontiersman, Boone was well schooled in the language and the customs of the Indians. It was said that he was one of the few white men who could outrival the red man in the native skills of endurance and cunning. It was fortunate for Boone that this was so, as he was captured by Indians several times but always managed to outwit them and escape.

On one such occasion, Boone escaped from the Indians and made his way back to Boonesboro just in time to warn the town and beat back an Indian attack which he'd learned about while in captivity.

But Daniel was not the only member of the Boone family to fall into Indian hands. On the quiet Sunday afternoon of July 14, 1776, Boone's two young daughters, Jemima and Fanny, along with another Boonesboro girl—sixteen-year-old Betsey Callaway—went canoeing on the river just below the frontier town.

The girls had not been on the water very long when their little craft was caught in a current and ran aground. As the three young friends attempted to free the canoe, a party of five Indians burst from the trees, swept up the frightened girls, and carried them off into the forest.

Sometime later that day the empty canoe drifted back to the settlement. Boone was told of the discovery and he at once suspected what had happened to Betsey and his daughters.

Immediately he organized a party of twenty armed men and set out in search of the missing girls. Although it was already growing dark, Boone and his posse plunged into the woods and soon picked up the Indians' trail.

Aware that they were being followed, the Indians split up the next morning and started off in three different directions, thus leaving three trails for their pursuers to puzzle over.

At first, Boone also divided his party and for several hours followed the divergent tracks. But they came up with nothing and Boone, suspecting a trick, decided to change his tactics.

Calling all his searchers back, Boone explained that he believed the Indians were purposely misleading them, that they were all headed for the same destination, a native village known to Boone and located deep in the forest. If the settlers abandoned the false trails set for them, said Boone, and headed instead directly for the village, they would arrive there before the Indians, as the progress of the kidnappers would be slowed up considerably by their struggling victims. By reaching the village first, the posse could await its quarry and take the Indians by surprise.

By midmorning of the following day, Boone's reasoning had proven to be correct and the gap between the pursuers and the pursued began to close rapidly. In fact, it closed too rapidly, because suddenly the search party found itself not ahead of but just on the heels of the kidnappers and the three girls. All were in a single group now and were heading, as Boone thought they would, for the tribal village.

Trailing them patiently, Boone awaited his opportunity. It came when the Indians stopped for their noon meal. At a signal from Boone, his companions silently closed in on the clearing in which the unsuspecting Indians had kindled their cooking fire.

With the camp surrounded, Boone prepared to launch a surprise attack. But before it could be executed, one anxious settler fired too soon and the Indians were alerted. Now there was no alternative. Rising from his hiding place, Boone took aim, fired, and brought down one of the captors. Another shot dropped a second Indian and then, in a volley of musket fire, the remaining three plunged into the woods.

The three girls, exhausted but safe, were led back to Boonesboro and the arms of their anxious families. And Boone's reputation as the equal of any Indian in cunning and tracking skill was once again proven.

Unfortunately, the great frontiersman's ability to outthink Indians was greater than his business acumen, and throughout his life Boone was in constant financial trouble.

Finally he lost everything. Then, stripped of his lands by his own government and feeling that the civilization he had been so instrumental in bringing west was smothering him, he decided once again to move on.

First it was to the area that became West Virginia. Later on he moved farther west, to what is now Missouri. There the years finally caught up with the legendary frontiersman. In 1820, this storied and generous man who had devoted so much of his life to the welfare of others died quietly while visiting one of his sons.

In 1845 his remains and those of Rebecca, his wife of sixty years, were returned from Missouri to Frankfort, Kentucky. There a monument commemorates the achievements of this remarkable American.

But Boone has another, greater monument. It is the fabled Wilderness Road which he built through the dense virgin forests of unexplored Kentucky in the 1770s.

This road, which followed the ancient trails of Indians and buffalo, became, for a full half-century, the main route for this young nation's westward expansion. Over Boone's rugged forest track moved a steady flow of men, women, children, and chattels, tens of thousands of hardy pioneers bound for new settlements.

Now paved, widened, and part of the great Dixie Highway, Boone's old road still exists. As it curves and dips and rises along its primitive ancestral route, the Wilderness Road is our nation's most enduring monument to its greatest frontiersman.

"Daniel Boone" U.S.A., 1968

Pollution—A Life Style

They died because of their cooking pots.

WE ARE ALL concerned about pollution today, but it is not a new menace. It is as old as the human race.

Man started to interfere with his environment from the moment he aspired to more than a simple animal existence and grabbed at the first rung of the upward mobility ladder. He's been going upward ever since, but at a price. For every sophisticated addition made to enhance his life style, man has created for himself a new problem. Generally, it's some form of pollution.

The creation of fire was certainly a supreme achievement; it gave feeble, fallible man the power of a god. It also led him inexorably to contamination of the earth's atmosphere through the uncontrolled burning of fuel.

Air pollution was noticed a long time ago. As far back as the sixteenth century, the English made legal reference to what must have been the equivalent of our modern smog. Noting that many London inhabitants were actually choking to death on the noxious fumes of combined sea-fog and smoke, the city fathers passed a series of strong laws against the use of soft smoke-producing fuel or faulty chimneys within the crowded confines of the town. These laws were implemented with heavy fines and—then as now—the threat to the purse did wonders toward cleaning up the city's foul air.

There are grim records of heavy penalties being meted out to polluters in even earlier times than those. In 1299, King Edward I of England had a man hanged for polluting the air with dense black smoke from a coal fire. This must have been an international problem because ten years later, in 1309, an Indian was hanged in Mexico City for polluting the air by burning charcoal. That's the same city which, today, has a higher carbon monoxide level than New York—and its high-altitude air contains more industrial contaminants than are found in the factory-crowded Rhine River valley.

Primitive man notably advanced himself when he first wore clothes and built a permanent shelter against the hostile elements. But these amenities bred a new kind of pollution for him. Unwittingly, in creating this "protected" environment, man also invited to live with him in warm intimate coziness a horde of smaller beings —the body louse, which was to give him the plague, and the flea-bearing rat, which brought him typhus.

How generous a host man was to these unwanted and contaminating little guests is graphically described by a medieval eyewitness to the funeral of the martyred Thomas à Becket, the English archbishop who was murdered in the Cathedral of Canterbury in December of 1170.

After his cruel death, the archbishop lay in the cathedral for some time, his body still clothed in the numerous garments of velvet, silk, and wool which he had worn both as a sign of his high office and for protection against the biting English winter.

As the archbishop's body grew cold, the creatures who had once flourished in the warmth of his clothing now deserted their host. And, notes a contemporary viewer of that incredible scene, as they left the dead man "the vermin boiled over like water in a simmering cauldron."

A great breakthrough for early agricultural man was the knowledge that excrement could be recycled through the soil to fertilize and enrich the crops which he had so recently learned to grow.

But, as usual, this progressive step encountered a painful thorn. Human waste made for abundant crops, all right, but it also caused the rapid growth of disease. It brought to towns and villages massive epidemics of deadly dysentry and cholera.

Such contamination of the environment was widespread. Sometimes, it changed the course of history.

In 1812, Napoleon was in command of a superb army of more than half a million healthy, well-trained men. With these, he left France and boldly marched across Europe to invade Russia and take Moscow.

In October of that same year Napoleon left Moscow, now a sacked and burnt-out city. But the master general did not leave in triumph as he had planned. Instead, he fled in panicky retreat, his once huge and seemingly invincible army reduced to eighty thousand sick and frightened men. Of these, less than twenty thousand ever made it back to their homes. They died like flies along the retreat route.

It was a disastrous defeat for Napoleon, but it was not caused by saber or cannon. The world's greatest military leader and his mighty army were routed by dysentry, typhus, all the killing diseases of man's own pollution.

An even greater historic event was caused by pollution of another kind.

Our ancestors learned early that there was more to eating than just berry picking, root grubbing, and making fateful decisions about wild mushrooms. They learned the art of cooking.

But the use of the skillet, like all other civilizing discoveries, proved to be a mixed blessing and brought man both joy and woe. In the case of Rome, it also brought national death.

The ancient Romans, it is now believed, helped to bring about the downfall of their great empire by cooking their sumptuous meals in pots made of lead— which leached out to contaminate the food that bubbled and simmered in the innocent-looking utensils. In time, this caused most of the Roman population to suffer from massive lead poisoning with its resulting mental and physical debility. Thus weakened, the empire became an easy target for enemies both within and without, and was lost forever.

So man-made pollution has been with us for a long time, shaping our lives or killing us off. It is a by-product of increasing civilization, and the problem will exist just as long as the human race survives on this crowded planet.

In fact, pollution seems to be the only single constant factor in man's ever-changing life style. Against it we must fight a ceaseless battle.

"Save Our Air" U.S.A., 1970

The Khyber Pass

It's the oldest and most carefully guarded trail in the world.

IT IS THE oldest, most continuously guarded trail in the world.

It is the famous Khyber Pass, the only land route from Central Asia to the subcontinent of India, a single natural rift through the towering peaks of the lonely Safed Koh Range which separates Afghanistan from Pakistan.

For more than three thousand years, through the Khyber's narrow thirty-three-mile length have passed the caravans of trade drawn by bullock, yak, camel, horse, and motor.

Over the dangerous pass have also come the famous conquerors of Asia. Alexander the Great, his soldiers mounted on swaying elephants, invaded India by way of the Khyber in the fourth century before Christ.

Later, the "White Huns" from the north poured through the Khyber gap to loot, burn, and kill under their leader Mihirakula, a man so cruel that he had his pack elephants toppled over the steep cliffs of the pass simply to see their mammoth suffering.

Through the Khyber Pass also came the forces of Mahmud of Ghazni, who brought his Islamic faith to divide Hindu India.

In the sixteenth century the walls of the Khyber echoed for the first time to the crash of artillery. That's when Babar, the Mongol invader, descendant of Genghis Khan, conquered India with the help of primitive cannon which fired huge round stones, forerunners of the iron ball.

Throughout the long, turbulent centuries, the Khyber has been guarded—officially and unofficially—by the same wild mountain tribesmen who watch over it today. Their purpose is to protect their own way of life, which is as ancient as the history of the pass itself. Tough fighters, superb horsemen, these fierce tribesmen make only one demand on all those who move over the Khyber: "Leave us alone!" In more than three thousand years, no one has ever routed them.

"Khyber Pass"   Pakistan, 1961

He Lit Up the World

"Only the wealthy will be able to burn candles."

WHEN THOMAS EDISON first visited Florida in 1885, the *Fort Myers Press* noted his arrival with this brief announcement: "Thomas A. Edison, electrician, is visiting here."

It was a curiously modest reference to the genius who even then, at age thirty-eight, was already world-famous and wealthy, with hundreds of patents to his credit. These ranged from the storage battery and the microphone to the incandescent lamp and the phonograph. Hidden still in the recesses of his amazing mind were inventions yet to come, inventions as diverse as the motion picture (a "talkie" was first projected by Edison on October 6, 1889) and a new method for concentrating iron ore.

In all, Edison was to chalk up a staggering record total of more than 1,300 patents, here and abroad, during his long lifetime. And one of his greatest inventions never was patented. That was the fluoroscope, which he left in public domain. He deemed the device too valuable to mankind for its use to be restricted in any way.

The amazing man who was to become wizard–midwife to the new age of instant sound and light had only three months of formal education. He was turned out of school at the age of seven on the grounds that he was difficult and unteachable: in short, a dummy.

Edison's father, owner of a lumber business at Port Huron, Michigan, and a political refugee from Canada (he had been an activist during the abortive attempt for home rule) did not make things easier for his small son. "My father," Edison once said, "thought I was stupid, and I almost decided I must be a dunce."

But Tom's mother, Nancy Edison, made no such judgment. The daughter of a Canadian Baptist minister, she was far ahead of her time in understanding her problem son. She decided that he was not slow, but that he was special. So she set out to help the troubled boy with long hours of patient teaching and unremitting love. Two years after she started her task, nine-year-old Tom had finished reading Gibbon's *Decline and Fall of the Roman Empire* and started on Parker's monumental *Natural and Experimental Philosophy*. The following year he built a simple laboratory in the cellar and began experiments in physics.

Of the remarkable woman who brought this miracle about, Edison would later say: "My mother . . . cast over me an influence which has lasted all of my life. The good effects of her early training I can never lose. If it had not been for her faith in me . . . I should very likely never have become an inventor."

He was a voracious reader all of his life. In his teens, Edison taught himself speed reading, practicing until he could read a whole line at a glance. "This faculty," he said later, "should be taught in all the schools—then one could read two or three books a day, whereas if only each word at a time is sensed then reading is laborious."

Edison invented the phonograph in 1877 and he kept a number of these big-horned machines around him at all times. This was always to be his favorite invention, although it had prevented him from being first with the telephone.

He was working on the telephone and had taken out a preliminary patent, when the idea of the "talking machine" suddenly came to him. He immediately set aside his telephonic experiments to concentrate on his new idea. This delay allowed Bell to come up with the communications wire first. But Bell's telephone was of no practical use—it could carry only a few miles—until Edison made it so with his invention of the carbon transmitter in 1878. This was actually the world's first microphone.

Edison's partiality for the phonograph may have been due to his deafness; he could hear the phonograph when he could hear nothing else.

His hearing had become seriously impaired at the age of twelve when he was working as a newsboy and candy butcher on the Grand Trunk Railway in Michigan. Trying to board a moving train one morning, his arms loaded with papers, he was swung aboard by a friendly conductor who grabbed the boy around his ears. "I felt something snap in my head," Edison recalled years afterward, "and the deafness started from that time and has progressed ever since."

Late in life, when he was almost totally deaf, Edison could still "hear" his beloved phonograph, and he could even tell when the sound of a new recording wasn't true.

To do this he bit lightly down on the instrument's wooden frame and with his teeth picked up the vibrations made by the recording. These impulses would then flow up through the delicate face bones and register on his sensitive inner ear.

Despite his increasing deafness, Edison loved to listen to music, which he believed was "next to religion" in elevating the spirit of man. To make it more enjoyable, he anticipated the high fidelity of modern stereo way back in 1905 when he attached two horns and two reproducers, set only fractions of an inch apart, to one of his machines.

All his life Edison was plagued by poor health, and it was on the advice of his doctors that he first went to Florida. The climate seemed to restore him, and the following winter he returned to Fort Myers.

Edison had been a widower on his first visit, but in 1886 he brought with him a bride. Her name was Mina Miller, and she was bright, brunette, and very pretty. She was also twenty years younger than her celebrated husband. But despite the wide difference in their ages, Mina and Tom were to share a tender love affair that spanned almost half a century, produced three lively children, and was broken only by death.

Soon after their marriage, Edison bought fourteen acres on the beautiful Caloosahatchee River at Fort Myers. There he built his famous Seminole Lodge which, through the years, was to become a mecca for the great names in the worlds of science and industry.

Actually, Seminole Lodge—which stands today just as Edison built it more than ninety years ago—consists of two identical houses. In one Edison worked and slept; the other contained the kitchen, dining room, and guest rooms.

The reason for the two houses was that Edison found irksome both the smell of cooking (he ate very little) and the conversation of guests who stayed too long. At that time the only way in or out of Fort Myers was by water. As passenger boats made only infrequent calls at the town, visitors who came to Seminole Lodge had to be put up—and put up with—for long periods of time.

Seminole Lodge, constructed of fine northern spruce, was built from Edison's own plans by a builder in Maine. Made up into sections and sent down by sea, the two dwellings were assembled and erected at Fort Myers by local workmen. This makes them the first prefabs ever built in this country.

Needless to say, the electrical equipment at Seminole was the most modern in the land. Electricity, after all, was Edison's abiding love. He once told a friend: "Just wait a little and we'll make electric light so cheap that only the wealthy will be able to burn candles."

Electric power was still not cheap in the 1880s, but plenty of it was generated at Seminole. When most of the world had yet to see even a light bulb, Edison had them blinking on and off automatically at the swing of a closet door. Electricity also sparked an intercom system which sometimes frightened unsophisticated visitors.

All power lines at Seminole were laid underground, enclosed in lead cables. These circuits still work efficiently, as do the vapor-proof switches which Edison placed outdoors to light up paths, trees, and his artesian-well swimming pool.

The pool was built for the Edison children and guests. Tom Edison did not use it. Although he took an annual camping trip into the Everglades for many years, the inventor did not like exercise and said so. When not absorbed in his work, he preferred to nap or double up with a book.

It was at his Fort Myers laboratory that Edison worked out one of his last experiments.

As early as 1918, the inventor believed that one day the United States would go to war against Japan, and that when this happened we would be cut off entirely from all our Asian sources of crude rubber. So Edison set out to find a new type of rubber to be made from native American plants.

In all, he experimented with seventeen thousand plants and finally decided that goldenrod, which grows in abundance here, could be processed to yield a natural rubber. From one acre of goldenrod he was able to produce more than one hundred pounds of latex. He turned his findings over to the government and, during World War II, a federal operation was set up in Louisiana which successfully turned out belting, tubes, and other needed products made from goldenrod rubber.

Today, clumps of Edison's goldenrod, growing to a height of fourteen feet, can still be seen at Seminole. Along with these are the stands of bamboo from whose carbonized fibers Edison once made the delicate filaments for his early electric lamps.

As the years rolled along, Edison spent more and more time at Fort Myers. Work was leavened with relaxation, part of this supplied by Edison's lifelong fondness for practical jokes.

Once a visitor to Seminole Lodge said that he liked everything about Florida except its beef. "Tough as leather," complained the guest.

Edison vigorously defended the local provender and then went off, found a piece of leather, brought it back to his cook, and had her cover it with gravy and garnishes.

At dinner that night the guest was served this tasty "steak." As his host extolled its flavor and tenderness, the man tried with desperate embarrassment to cut it.

Only when Edison reeled from the table, helpless with laughter, did the visitor realize that he'd been the butt of a culinary joke.

Thomas Edison died on October 18, 1931. He was eighty-four years old and had been a prime force in turning the world around. Up until the very end, with the always frail body now further ravaged by several wasting diseases, the questing mind continued on, darting tirelessly along the avenues of creation.

Shortly before his passing, Edison told a friend that he had a notebook filled with experiments that would keep a man busy for a century. He was still adding to this when death came to extinguish the life of the man who had lit up the world.

"Thomas Edison"   U.S.A., 1947

The Mark of Mercy

All men, in all wars, honor this familiar
banner.

OF ALL ILLUSTRATIONS ever seen on stamps, the one on
the stamp shown here is the most universal. It is the
familiar banner of the Red Cross and it has appeared
on the stamps of more nations than any other single
symbol.

It all started a little over a century ago when a young
Swiss named Jean Henri Dunant was an observer at an
unusually bloody battle between the French and the
Austrians at the little town of Solferino in Italy.

The furious battle—which left thirty thousand men
dead and wounded in a short space of time—was so
shocking that both sides withdrew, and soon after a
peace was arranged between them.

The terrible sight of the wounded lying agonized and untended where they had fallen stirred Dunant deeply. Later, back in Switzerland, he wrote a book about his experiences and made a public plea for some system to be organized to help the pitiful casualties of war as they dropped, wounded or dying, on the battlefield.

Dunant's story aroused immediate public interest and in 1864 the historic Geneva Convention met in that Swiss city and formed what we now call the Red Cross. At that time, the Convention also laid down the rules for neutrality to protect those brave men and women who go to the aid of battlefield casualties. Those rules, now internationally accepted, are still in force.

Because Dunant was the true founder of this humanitarian movement, the Convention honored him by choosing his country's flag—a white cross on a red field—as its symbol. However, when it was pointed out that this might be an embarrassment should Switzerland ever go to war, it was decided to use the Swiss national emblem of a cross, but to reverse the colors. So the Red Cross flag was born.

In a few countries, for religious reasons, a red crescent took the place of the red cross. But whichever emblem is used, it is still honored thoughout the world as the mark of mercy.

"Swiss and Red Cross Emblems"   *Switzerland, 1957*

The World's Most Unusual Diamond

It's a gem so strange that no value can be set upon it.

MANY REGIONS OF Africa are rich in diamonds—the gems men have fought over and died for ever since they started to adorn themselves and their women with the minerals of the earth.

Among the countries that mine these icy beauties, South Africa is foremost in the production of fine gem stones. In the little republic of Sierra Leone, however, diamonds are found in such abundance that they make up the country's chief export. Mostly these are industrial diamonds, but recently a high-quality diamond was found there which weighed in at 969.8 carats. That's about the size of an egg, and is now the largest diamond in the world.

But it is not the largest ever found. That was the famous Cullinan diamond, which was discovered at the

Premier Mine in South Africa in 1905 and was presented to King Edward VII of England for the royal jewel collection. When it was first found, before cutting, it was the width of a man's hand and weighed over three thousand carats.

No question about it, these monster diamonds are marvels among jewels. But there is another kind of gem-stone wonder. It is the smallest diamond in the world, a little beauty weighing in at the eyeball-popping size of just 1/800 of 1 carat, tinier than the dot over this "i."

I first saw this amazing stone a few years ago when I was in Amsterdam, Holland, to get a story about diamond making. I had arranged to interview Herman Van Moppes, the great-great-grandson of the founder of what is now the largest diamond "factory" in existence.

To acquaint me with the various phases of diamond cutting, Van Moppes took me on a tour of his workrooms. We had gone through a number of these, all filled with skilled craftsmen bent over their delicate task of transforming dingy chunks of rough diamonds into gem stones, when we came to a small room where there was a display of some elaborate jewelry. With this was a microscope, the ordinary kind found in any medical laboratory.

Van Moppes directed my attention to the microscope. "Have a look in there," he said.

I bent over the instrument and looked down the barrel. Beneath the lens, winking up at me from the metal platform used to hold slides, was a perfect little diamond. It was a flawless blue-white beauty, gleaming from all its fifty-eight facets—the full traditional number of "sides" for a true brilliant.

I was seeing, Van Moppes informed me, the smallest perfectly cut and polished stone that man had ever created. It was about the size of a grain of sand. Now, under the powerful lens, I was viewing the little gem magnified 630 times.

To achieve this spectacular feat of miniaturization, Van Moppes had to design new infinitesimally small tools and disks for the difficult operation, equip them with magnifying lenses, and build a special dust-free booth in which the work could be done.

When everything was ready, the rough stone was carefully chosen—a tiny blue-white diamond perfect in color and texture. Then the difficult, painstaking task of cutting it was entrusted to four of the company's most experienced craftsmen, each an expert in a single phase of diamond making.

"It took three months to finish the diamond," Van Moppes explained. "The men could only work on it for short periods of time. It was hard on their eyes and very difficult for their nerves because of its size. It gave them the jitters. The final polishing alone took three weeks and the man who did it collapsed when it was all over. We had to send him off on a long holiday to rest."

I thought of the hazards involved in forming the stone. "Did the little diamond ever slip from its delicate holder during the process?" I asked.

Van Moppes smiled in rueful memory.

"Indeed it did. It was 'lost' sixteen times. Each time it fell we went over the special booth with a magnifying glass. Sometimes, it didn't show up. When that happened, we carefully cleaned the floor of the booth by hand and gathered up perhaps a thimbleful of dust. We then placed this little heap of sweepings on a plate, sprinkled it with a drop of gasoline, and set it on fire. In the intense heat, everything burned away except that morsel of pure carbon which was our little lost diamond."

Fascinated by the remarkable stone and knowing that others would be also, I suggested to Van Moppes that he lend it to me for use on a television program I knew I could set up. Under special magnification, millions could then see the unique stone.

Van Moppes agreed to let me have the diamond. It would have to travel, of course, securely taped in its microscope. Removing it would be too chancy.

Well, the little stone flew the Atlantic and reached Kennedy Airport all right, but it never did appear on television.

The United States customs, puzzled by this tiny gem which had at once no value by weight but great value because of its rarity, could fix no duty on it. Even a diamond expert from Cartier's who went out to view the stone at Kennedy, where it was being held, could give no opinion as to its worth.

So the Van Moppes diamond was held in customs for months, while the date arranged for its appearance on television came and passed. Then, with everyone weary of the delay, I held a series of talks with customs, a special token duty was finally agreed upon, and the minute diamond fixed to its microscope was released to me at last.

A photograph of the diamond had never been made, so I arranged to have it sent to Rochester, New York, where Kodak, with the aid of magnifying equipment it uses for medical research, made an excellent picture of the rare stone. It is shown blown up to thousands of times its original size.

At present the Van Moppes diamond, with its faithful microscope, rests safely in a bank vault, a mighty mite of the mineral world, as amazing in its own right as any of its famous giant sister stones.

"Diamond"   *South Africa, 1965*

The First Stamp Collector

It started with wallpaper for a girl's room.

ON MAY 1, 1840, thousands of Londoners flocked to the General Post Office to buy up some of the new postal curiosities. These had just gone on sale that day for the first time anywhere and were, as the press reported, "bits of paper covered at the back with a glutinous wash." They also bore the profile of young Queen Victoria and sold for a penny and a halfpenny.

These were, of course, the world's first postage stamps. And hard on their heels came the world's first stamp collector. She surfaced in 1841 through an ad which appeared in the *London Times*. It read:

A young lady, being desirous of covering her dressing room with canceled postage stamps, has so far been encouraged in her wish by private friends as to have succeeded in collecting 16,000. These, however, being insufficient, we will greatly be obliged if any good-natured person who may have these (otherwise useless) articles at their disposal, would assist her in her whimsical project. Address: E.D., Mr. Butt's, Gover, Leadenhall Street; or Mr. Marshall's, Jeweler, Hackney.

The stamps sought by this "whimsical" little lady ould have been the Penny Black and the Two Pence lue, the first stamps issued by England. Both of these re now rare stamps and, at a conservative guess, the allpaper for that girl's room would now run her about 500 for the square inch.

A lot has happened since that ad appeared almost a ntury and a half ago. Every country now issues post-ge stamps and every country now has a horde of stamp llectors. No one knows exactly how many there are it an educated guess places the total at upwards of a ndred million, with about fifteen million collectors in e United States alone.

Stamp collecting—or "philately" as the Frenchman erpin named the hobby in 1864—is today a very mplex and specialized pursuit. Stamps cascade off e international presses in the multibillion sheets an-ally, and they feature thousands of different subjects. single private collector could hope to keep up with e stamps of the world.

That is why most collectors now restrict themselves single subjects. They collect, for instance, only mps of certain periods, or of dogs, or flags, or tional heroes, or of art reproductions, or flowers. One man has a large collection of only one flower, the s.

Other collectors specialize in different ways. They

acquire only such items as first day covers, air mail stamps, postal cards, or plate blocks (sheets of stamps bearing serial numbers). Some even collect only stamps of irregular shape, although there are not too many of these.

Almost all stamps are four-sided. This is because it is a convenient shape for printing in large sheets; it is also cheaper. But there have been departures in form.

The first odd-shaped stamps to appear were the Cape of Good Hope Triangles printed in South Africa in the early 1860s. Today one of these rare triangles will fetch as much as $4,000 or more on the stamp market.

A century later, in 1964, another African country, the little diamond-rich Sierra Leone, made postal history by issuing the first free-form stamp, shaped like the map of the country. It was also the first self-adhesive stamp ever issued.

At almost the same time, the South Sea kingdom of Tonga prepared its own surprise for the stamp world. In 1962 Tonga, which was then ruled by its majestic six-foot-two-inch Queen Salote, put into public circulation the first gold coins ever minted in Polynesia. A year later, to commemorate this new coinage, Tonga issued the first round stamps (like coins) ever printed —and had them embossed on gold leaf. Following this philatelic coup, Queen Salote issued another first in 1964, a heart-shaped stamp also printed on gold leaf. Nothing else like these stamps has ever been seen by collectors.

Some stamps arouse interest because they have stirred controversy, like the United States "Love" stamp of 1973.

This was issued as a light touch in philately, and was meant to be used on love letters and other sentimental mailings. But thousands of letter writers interpreted the stamp's message differently, and they flooded the postmaster general's office with their tart, unloving comments. The stamp, they wrote, promoted a "hippy" philosophy . . . it encouraged permissiveness . . . it even hinted at free love.

Of course, it did none of these things and, despite the criticism, the stamp sold well. Apparently "love" is still a nice word for a lot of people.

A different kind of controversy occurred when the little South American republic of Guyana issued a Christmas stamp in 1967. For some reason not quite clear, the holiday stamp bore the likeness of Cussin' Millie, a nationally famous macaw noted for its salty bilingual swearing. When the stamp went on sale, thousands of irate Guyanans wrote to their Communications Director denouncing the stamp. They were backed up by a leading local newspaper which in a sizzling front page editorial warned that "to commemorate Christmas with Millie is the ultimate blasphemy." But it was too late to recall the protested stamps, and so Millie the Macaw stayed for the holidays.

Stamp collectors have sharp eyes, especially for errors.

A schoolboy collector in Cranston, Rhode Island, spotted a mistake in the flag shown on top of the *Mayflower* in the "Landing of the Pilgrims" stamp, a commemorative issued in 1970. Writing the postmaster general, the observant youngster pointed out that the *Mayflower* flag had too many red stripes on it. The postmaster admitted the error and sent the boy a letter of special commendation.

When the illustration for the Boston Tea Party stamp was finished, a collector noticed that the crescent of the moon did not conform with the time of the tea toss into Boston Harbor. So back to the drawing board went the artist, and another stamp error was averted.

One stamp error wound up in court.

In 1962, the Panama Canal Zone issued a stamp commemorating its new Thatcher Ferry Bridge. To make the bridge stand out, it was overprinted on the basic stamp in silver ink. At one point, this metallic inking failed and a number of stamps were printed with no bridge spanning the river. The error was quickly corrected, but some of these stamps got into circulation. These immediately became rarities and were sought after by collectors.

However, the post office did not want these few hundred stamps to become so valuable, and announced that it would print thousands of the stamps without the bridge. By making them commonplace, the stamps would become valueless for collectors. (The post office had taken similar action in the case of a previous misprint on its Dag Hammarskjöld stamp.)

But this was not done. Instead, a Boston stamp dealer, Henry Harris, went to court to restrain the post office from deliberately misprinting a stamp issue. Harris won his case and today the Thatcher Ferry Bridge rarity is valued at $3,000.

Many stamp errors are due to inversions. This means that part of a stamp has been printed upside down. Generally, it is the center.

A record for center inversions was made by the United States in 1869 when four stamps in one series were found misprinted. On one of these stamps, Lincoln's portrait appeared upside down; on another, two flags flew in the wrong direction. On the third stamp—the "Signing of the Declaration of Independence"—all the signers stood on their heads. And the fourth stamp had Columbus landing in the New World with the shore suspended above him. The Lincoln error was caught in time and the stamps held back. But the other three inversions went into circulation. Today they are all valued in the many thousands of dollars.

In 1901, three more inversions occurred in a series commemorating the Pan American Exposition. In these stamps, a lake steamer, an electric car, and a train are all shown traveling on their tops. The current values of these inversions range all the way from $6,000 to $21,000.

All inversions are valuable, of course, but the most famous is the one known as the 24-cent Air Mail Invert.

In 1918, the United States issued its first air mail stamps. During the printing of these 24-cent stamps, the plane in the center was briefly printed upside down. The error was corrected but a hundred-stamp sheet (or pane, as philatelists call these) leaked out. By chance, this was bought by W. T. Robey, a Washington stamp collector who later sold the stamps for $15,000. Today, the 24-cent Air Mail Invert is one of the world's rarest stamps and is valued at $47,500.

It is clear that stamp collecting is not only a fascinating hobby, it can also be a very lucrative one.

"Stamp Collecting"   *U.S.A., 1972*

Women at War

In blue and in olive drab, they went to war—like "soldier" Sampson before them.

It was not until the mid-twentieth century that American women officially went to war. Then, quickly but superbly trained, the Wacs and Waves went off by the tens of thousands to help win World War II.

For the first time in our history, uniformed women fully shared the military life and duties of their brothers and husbands. Except for actual combat, they went wherever the battles were being fought, to do the jobs that only fighting men had done before.

Women were called to all branches of the service. In crisp designer-tailored uniforms, perky hats set at a jaunty angle, they served in the army, navy, air corps, and marines. Women piloted transport planes and acted as orderlies. They repaired jeep engines and risked their lives as couriers. They were company clerks and paymasters and commissioned officers. They worked in communications, sat in at staff meetings, policed barracks, and performed legal work. They were bright, dedicated soldiers, part of a great fighting force, and many of them never returned home.

The women of World War II had a solid tradition to go on. Their sisters before them had been helping to win our wars ever since Revolutionary times.

It was a young girl, Sybil Ludington, who rode all night through the Connecticut countryside to call out the local minutemen and defeat a surprise attack by the British in 1776.

It was feisty "Molly Pitcher"—Molly Hayes, really—who risked death and won her curious name by carrying water to cool the men and the guns of her husband's battery at the Battle of Monmouth in 1778.

Brave Margaret Corbin did even more. When her husband fell dead beside his cannon during the disastrous British attack on Fort Washington in 1776, Margaret sprang to take his place. In a battle noted for its savagery, she continued loading and firing her husband's cannon until, badly wounded herself, she was carried from her post.

Margaret's supreme courage did not go unrecognized. She was the first woman ever to receive a pension from our government, and her memory has been uniquely honored with a monument at West Point.

And then there was that "first authentic female soldier," Deborah Sampson. Deborah was a twenty-two-year-old Massachusetts girl who walked into the recruiting center at Worcester one spring day in 1782 and offered her services to "fight the British."

They were readily accepted—because the tall plain-faced country girl, dressed in a man's shapeless homespun, her hair cropped and her bosom tightly strapped down, had neglected to mention her sex. Enlisting under the improvised name of Robert Shurtleff, the new recruit fooled everyone and was promptly attached to the Fourth Massachusetts Foot Regiment.

Soon after young "Soldier Shurtleff" joined up, the Massachusetts Fourth started on a long, hard march to the Revolutionary camp at West Point, in New York.

Even at these close quarters, none of the men in her regiment ever suspected that an amazon was among them. Instead, they found her an excellent soldier, if a little reserved in her habits.

Deborah received her baptism of fire at Tappan Bay on the Hudson, when she was slashed by an enemy saber during a hand-to-hand encounter. Recovering from this, she later stopped a musket ball at what is now Eastchester, New York.

This wound was of a more intimate nature than the saber cut. Fearing discovery of her secret, Deborah refused help from the company surgeon and took to the woods. There she hid out until she had nursed herself back to health.

With the musket ball still in her body (she was to carry it all her life), Deborah then rejoined her comrades and engaged in fresh action.

Her military conduct was outstanding. This brought her to the attention of her officers and she was tapped as an orderly on the staff of General Patterson in Philadelphia. The post was an honor, of course, but it proved Deborah's undoing.

Shortly after she arrived in the City of Brotherly Love, an epidemic of yellow fever struck. Deborah fell victim to the disease, sank into a coma, and was judged a goner.

Taken to a hospital ward reserved for hopeless cases, she was given a final medical check to see if any life existed. A doctor, unbuttoning Deborah's army shirt to listen for a heartbeat, quickly uncovered the secret which the girl-soldier had kept hidden for so long.

Deborah recovered from the fever, was honored for her military record by a parade at West Point, and was given an honorable discharge. Later, she also received a military pension—eight dollars a month for life.

After her discharge, Deborah fell in love with Benjamin Gannett, married, had three lively children, and settled down in Sharon, Massachusetts, to the hardworking life of an early American housewife.

Deborah Sampson Gannett died on April 29, 1827, at the age of sixty-seven. During World War II, a Liberty Ship was named in her honor.

"Women in the Armed Services"   *U.S.A., 1952*

It Makes the World
Go 'Round

Or, as Publilius Syrus first phrased it 2,300 years ago: "Money alone sets all the world in motion."

COINS AND MONEY are not usual subjects for a special issue of stamps, but the Greeks have good reason to take pride in their coins, like the one shown on this stamp. Greek coins were among the most beautiful produced by the ancient peoples.

Greek coinage started early. Although silver and gold were also used, Homer mentions that brass coins were current among the Greeks as early as 1184 B.C. Earlier still, copper nails were accepted as currency in some parts of Greece.

The Greeks did not initiate the use of metal for money, however. That was done by the people of Lydia, a small but enormously rich nation in Asia

Minor. They were the first to put metal currency into popular use—about 2,500 years ago.

The most ancient coins are all made of electrum, a combination of four parts gold to one part silver. But the most famous of all ancient coins was made of a much humbler substance. I have one of these old coins; it is the "widow's mite."

The mite is immortalized in the Bible. In the twelfth chapter of Mark we learn the true spirit of sharing through the touching parable of the poor widow who gave "two mites" so that others could be helped.

The mite was a tiny coin crudely made of copper, and of the lowest value. It was used in Judea, formerly Judah, a small kingdom in the southern part of Palestine.

Once copper had formed the basis of ancient currency but, in time, this metal gave way to silver and gold. The Biblical poor, however, rarely saw the Hebrew silver shekel or the Roman silver penny, called the denarius. As for the gold coins of that day, the impoverished never even knew they existed.

So copper, almost valueless, became the common coinage of the poor.

Currency, its value and form, is constantly changing to keep pace with the times. During the thousands of years it's been around, it has been made from many things.

Leather was used for money in ancient Carthage, and it was used again in Austria as late as 1933.

Wampum (bead money) fueled our early fur trade, and tobacco was declared legal tender in Maryland in 1639. In the Solomon Islands you can still buy coconuts with porpoise teeth, and China once used salt for cash. In Mexico during the last century, bars of soap were sometimes taken as currency. And the Germans once even tried porcelain coins.

The stone money of the island of Yap, in the South Pacific, defies any change purse. It is called "fei" and consists of limestone disks from six inches up to twelve feet across, depending on value. This mighty currency is accepted by the natives of Yap, and a twenty-inch disk is said to be enough to buy a large pig or a young wife.

Sweden holds the record for making the largest and heaviest metal coin. It was the ten-daler piece, and it was minted in 1644. The huge coin weighed forty-seven pounds and shaped up to a big rectangle of twelve by twenty-seven inches. Its value was about $100, a very large sum at that time. The coin was made of copper, which Sweden then had in abundance. Later the copper value exceeded the monetary value and the outsized currency was eventually sold for its metal content.

You can still buy something for a square nickel, the only coin of its kind in the world.

In 1910, the Dutch government decided that their round nickel caused too much confusion with a similar coin valued at twenty-five cents. So its shape was changed into a square. Eventually the square nickel dropped out of use in Holland, but it is still used in the Dutch West Indies, although it is becoming rare there also.

The strangest money surfaced about three centuries ago.

In 1685 the French king was short of funds and unable to pay his troops stationed in Canada. Because there was no paper in the colony on which to print local currency, the military governor of Canada requisitioned all available playing cards and used their backs as banknotes. This use of cards for currency continued for several decades.

In the United States, the first Federal coins were

issued from our brand new mint in Philadelphia in October, 1792. As there was a shortage of gold and silver at the time, the mint issued only copper coins—pennies and halfpennies.

Two years later the first silver dollars left the mint. They caused a storm of controversy because they bore the figure of an eagle. Many felt that the eagle—often a symbol of monarchy—should not be used by a people who had just thrown off a kingly yoke.

The Federal coins were not the first struck in this country. The earliest coins were issued by a mint near Boston in 1652. They were silver shillings and sixpence and threepence pieces. But these coins had no distinguishing design and had to be replaced with more distinctive ones (the Willow Tree) because the original coins were so easily counterfeited.

Counterfeiting, of course, poses a great threat to a nation's currency. And to a nation.

A flood of useless colonial paper money, extensively counterfeited by the British during the Revolution, almost lost us the war. It caused panic among the people and shook their faith in the newly formed government in Philadelphia. Washington named counterfeiting as one of his most dangerous foes.

The first known case of counterfeiting in this country occurred in 1699 when a Connecticut man by the name of Robert Fenton was accused of making and passing bogus coins.

Later, during the American Revolution, counterfeiting was so widespread that a law was passed making the crime equal to treason and punishable by death.

But the death penalty did not deter the more daring of the funny-money men who continued to pursue their dangerous but lucrative art. Later, when the death penalty was lifted, counterfeiters became even bolder and more numerous.

To combat this unhealthy trend in the economy, Federal laws were passed which gave the Treasury Department broad powers with which to move against counterfeiters. The enforcement of one of these laws led to an amazing penalty against a famous American artist.

He was Charles Meurer, an Ohio man who entered one of his celebrated paintings for exhibition at the Chicago World's Fair in 1893. Meurer's painting, a large canvas entitled *My Passport,* showed among other items in the background three American bills of different denominations. All the bills were meticulously painted from the originals and were exact copies down to the last detail.

This artistic precision was the painting's downfall. A few days after it was hung, the Federal government moved in and confiscated the canvas on the charge that it violated the law against illegal reproduction of United States currency. No American currency, stated the law, could be exactly duplicated for any reason at all.

Eventually the painting was returned to the artist, but not before something new had been added. Across the face of each bill on the canvas a cautious Treasury Department had carefully drawn several fine red lines.

"Zeus and Eagle—Ancient Coin" Greece, 1959

The Power of One Vote

A single vote saved the presidency from dishonor; another set the world on fire.

THE MOST POWERFUL weapon that free men possess is the ballot. By using it, you can shape the future. The destinies of men and nations throughout history have been changed because just one important vote was cast . . . or not cast.

In March, 1868, the greatest political trial in the history of our country began when impeachment proceedings were brought against Andrew Johnson, the Tennessee tailor who, upon the tragic death of Lincoln, had become the seventeenth president of the United States. Johnson was charged with the grave national crime of abusing his executive powers and went on trial before the Senate, which in such cases sits as both judge and jury. After a lengthy hearing a vote finally was taken among the senators and Johnson was found innocent by the narrow margin of just one ballot.

This historic single vote not only saved our highest office from dishonor and shame, it also prevented a serious miscarriage of justice. It is believed today that Andrew Johnson was the innocent victim of politics.

On October 18, 1867, at the city of New Archangel (now called Sitka), the territory known as Russian America became American-owned Alaska. Secretary of State William Seward, who almost alone foresaw the great future of this territory, had worked out the purchase treaty with Baron Steeckel, Russian minister to the United States. And Seward had worked out a bargain price, too. For this rich northern land we paid only $7,200,000—about two cents an acre.

At that time most congressmen thought the Alaska purchase a foolish one. They jeered at it as "Seward's Folly" and called Alaska "Seward's Icebox." So when Seward presented his treaty to the Senate for ratification, there was loud debate against it. But Seward hammered away at the value of Alaska, and finally he persuaded a reluctant Senate to agree to its purchase.

The Alaska purchase was ratified by just one vote. And by that vote we acquired the territory that was to become our largest state—more than twice the size of Texas—and a potential powerhouse of resources.

In the election of 1800, Thomas Jefferson and Aaron Burr tied in the Electoral College for the presidency—seventy-three to seventy-three. The election was then thrown into the House of Representatives where it would be decided by a simple majority as provided by law.

Following a long deadlock, during which ballots were cast thirty-six separate times—resulting in thirty-six separate ties—Jefferson finally won. This was after Alexander Hamilton, head of the opposing Federalist Party, persuaded a Federalist legislator to change his vote in favor of Jefferson on the ground that he was a less dangerous man than Burr. This behind-the-scenes breakthrough brought other Federalists into Jefferson's camp and on the final ballot he was elected president by a clear margin. Burr then became vice president.

But these king-making activities on the part of Hamilton brought him eventual disaster. A few years after this presidential election, Burr ran for the governorship of New York. Again Hamilton used his great political power to thwart his detested opponent. And again Burr lost. Furious, Burr challenged Hamilton to a duel. Hamilton accepted and was killed.

Right after World War I, a young German soldier who had recently been demobilized made his way to the city of Munich. There he decided to settle and, for a while, he made a modest living by painting commercial posters. But like many others in that postwar era, he was bitter and discontented with his lot, so he joined a small political group of dissidents which had just been formed. The group expanded rapidly and so did the young soldier's reputation within it. Finally, it was felt that the time had come when this new organization could make a decisive movement against the legal government of Germany. On November 8, 1923, at a Munich beer hall called the Burgerbrau Keller, this new revolutionary party held a hurried meeting to elect a leader. By a majority of one single vote they chose the ex-soldier.

The rest, of course, is history. For that obscure

soldier was none other than Adolph Hitler, the man whose evil destiny it was to set the whole world on fire.

Patrick Henry, great patriot of the American Revolution, took the first step toward freedom and independence for his land when he rose before the Virginia Assembly to defy the legality of the hated Stamp Act. This act had been imposed on the colonies by King George to raise money for the maintenance of his troops on this soil.

On a historic day in May, 1765, the fiery young lawyer read his now-famous resolution that no one but Viginians could impose taxation on Virginia. The colony, he said, need not obey this illegal law of the king's. There were many aristocrats present in the Assembly that day, and at these shocking words they arose in anger with cries of "treason," a very serious charge at any time.

"Many threats were uttered and much abuse was cast on me," Henry wrote later, but he persisted in reading his resolution to the end. Then, facing the Assembly, he said: "If this be treason, make the most of it."

Patrick Henry's resolution, the first toward American independence, was passed that fateful day by the margin of just one single vote.

The closest election in the United States was lost not by one vote, but by one-sixth of a vote. That was in 1872 when Francis Marion Cockrell ran against Charles H. Hardin for the governorship of Missouri. In those days, each county in Missouri with a population of five hundred or over was represented by one delegate. Counties with fewer than five hundred people had their representation prorated. As Missouri was then pioneer country and sparsely settled, several counties had fewer than one hundred inhabitants. These were entitled to only one-sixth of a vote.

The election was a tie all the way, but finally Cockrell failed to carry just one of these almost uninhabited counties and lost the governorship of Missouri by the margin of just one-sixth of a vote—the narrowest margin in election history.

"Register—Vote" U.S.A., 1968

The Alaskan Called
Soapy Smith

The most famous folk figure of the Alaska Territory, he became a legend in his own time.

THE PURCHASE OF the Alaska Territory in 1867 was one of the greatest real estate deals of all time. Without a shot being fired, and at the bargain price of only two cents an acre, we became overnight the owners of a chunk of land more than twice the size of Texas.

Along with the territory came a lot of dividends . . . abundant wildlife, spectacular scenery, virgin forests, an untapped treasury of vast mineral wealth, and the highest mountain on the continent, Mount McKinley. In addition, there was the awesome Valley of Ten Thousand Smokes, rocks that are feather-light, giant brown bears, magnificent hundred-foot totem poles, and Sitka, the only "Russian" town in the country.

Eventually, the Alaska Territory also gave us something more—Soapy Smith, one of the greatest folk figures in our history. A notorious badman during territorial days, Soapy is a household word among Alaskans.

I first heard about Soapy a long while ago, when I was a schoolboy. My father, a New York doctor, had taken me on an Alaskan junket which retraced the steps of the old sourdoughs of the gold rush days. Naturally, this took us to Skagway which, in its heyday, had been the gateway to Canada's gold-rich Yukon Territory.

For a while, as gold poured out of the frozen north, Skagway boomed. By 1898 it had become the largest city in the Alaska Territory—a roaring, wide-open tent-and-shack city with a tough, ever-changing population of twenty thousand gold-fevered men and women.

But all that changed when the Klondike finally petered out. Then Skagway became what she was before the rush—a windswept, isolated little town hugging the shore of the Taiya Inlet.

Skagway is really a frontier town. It was when I first saw it, and it still is today (I went back there again just a few years ago). The town lies at the foot of brooding glacial peaks which cast long shadows over its small jumble of houses and shops, its wooden walkways, and the narrow unpaved streets which straggle off to nowhere.

There are only a few hundred people living in Skagway now, most of them born there from parents who were born there. The town's architecture is straight out of an old-timey western, and so is the local cemetery. It's a place out of the past, peopled by ghosts—lively ghosts from the gold rush days.

And chief among all these ghosts is Soapy Smith. A legend in his own brief time (he was dead at thirty-eight), Soapy's memory grows greener with the passing years. People spoke about him when I was a boy, and they still talk of him. He is all Alaska's favorite bad-man, but he is especially cherished in Skagway because that's where his turbulent life peaked and ended.

Soapy (born Jefferson Randolph Smith in Colorado) arrived in Skagway in 1896, shortly after the first news of the Klondike gold strike leaked out to the world.

He was then in his thirties, good looking, well groomed, and superbly skilled in duplicity. A thousand shady adventures in a hundred different towns had made him one of the greatest con men of his time.

Soapy had lived by his wits from early boyhood. While still in his teens he had acquired the nickname that was to be his for the rest of his life. It came by way of a variation that he made on the old shell game. Instead of bilking his victims by placing the "sucker money" under a nutshell, Soapy wrapped his lure around a cake of soap. He always claimed that his system was "cleaner." He was not without a sense of humor.

News of the gold strike told Soapy that his hour had finally come, that his talents could be fully used in the boom that was shaping up for Skagway. This isolated little inland port was the only feasible entrance to the Yukon Territory and the untapped riches of the Klon-dike. Through it would necessarily pass all the men and supplies headed for the gold fields. And back through Skagway, on their way out, would come these same men, their pokes now heavy with nuggets and glittering dust.

Soapy calculated to grab a good share of this raw wealth. So off to the North he trotted.

Not long after he arrived in Skagway, Soapy man-aged to make for himself a sizeable stake at the gam-bling tables, and when the gold rush got under way a few months later he was ready for it.

He had by then used his stake to invest in a palatial saloon which he named Jeff's Place, and he stocked this with lots of fire water, amiable women, and the latest in gambling machines—which he had fixed for the benefit of the house.

This business netted Soapy a large income, but he found still more ways of growing even richer.

He salted a number of mines and sold them for high sums to easily deceived fortune seekers. He made a tidy profit by turning supplier and overcharging miners who had to buy pack horses and load up at Skagway for the long, dangerous trek to the Klondike. (The Canadian government would not permit any prospector to cross the steep White Pass into the Yukon unless he had a ton of supplies with him.)

A contemporary invention helped Soapy to line his pockets further. He set up a phony telegraph service at Skagway and, for five dollars a throw plus distance charges, he tapped out messages to nowhere for gold hunters who thought they were sending home final words before hitting the trail.

As might be expected, because of the shady nature of these enterprises, Soapy also had carved several notches on his fine handmade gun by this time. He always claimed that he shot only in self-defense.

As Soapy's wealth increased so did his power, and it wasn't long before he had made himself a force in politics—or what passed for politics in booming Skagway with its large, tough, fluid population of gold seekers.

But it wasn't just money that gave Soapy his political clout. He also had that elusive something called charisma. Despite his notoriously bad habits, he was able to charm many of the locals. He had also gained a reputation for generosity and personal courage. Tales of his derring-do and of his gifts to orphans and "widder-women" proliferated like sourdoughs on the old Chilkoot Trail. Ballads were sung about him from Whitehorse to Seattle.

On the other hand, of course, there were still those whom Soapy failed to charm, bilked men who wanted to cut his black heart from his sturdy body. They contended Soapy was a bad influence on the whole territory, was a foe to decency, and that he had made himself "boss" of Skagway by means of money, guile, and lots of muscle.

It was true that Soapy's "persuaders" were everywhere, a mixed bag of fugitives, bunco artists, and itinerant gunmen. With their help, Soapy did maintain a corrupt grip on Skagway. But it was a town whose moral tone was at best only a neutral gray, and nobody seemed to mind the bossism too much.

So despite the complainers, that's how things stood for a while. Then, early in 1898, a group of honest citizens organized for reform. Calling themselves the Committee of 101, they vowed to run Soapy and his thugs out of Skagway.

In reply to this threat, Soapy laughed, organized a Committee of 303 (in a show of comparative strength), and loudly let it be known that he was staying on as boss of Skagway.

Well, Soapy was right. He did stay, and forever.

On July 8, 1898, when the gold rush was at its height, word reached Soapy at his saloon that the party opposing him was having a secret meeting down on a local wharf. The object was to get rid of Soapy immediately.

Always one to take direct action, Soapy collected his bodyguards and, armed and confident, he strode down to the night-darkened water. On the wharf Soapy encountered a man named Reid who was acting as a lookout for the meeting. There were a few sharp words, and then Soapy pulled his gun and shot Reid at close range. As the lookout dropped, there was the crack of another shot and Soapy took a fatal bullet in his chest.

It was said that both men had killed each other, Reid firing as he fell. But the bullet removed from Soapy at the improvised morgue that night did not match Reid's gun. Nor did the position of the wound make any sense. The two men had been facing each other when the fatal shots were fired, but the bullet which stopped Soapy's heart had entered directly into his side.

To this day no one knows who killed Soapy Smith. But it doesn't really matter. It just adds an extra touch of mystery and color to the legend of Alaska's most notorious badman, who has lain for almost eighty years in the little "boot hill" cemetery at Skagway.

"Alaska Territory" U.S.A., 1937

The World's Most Popular Pet

Elegant, aloof, and mysterious, they were frequently symbols of religion.

PROBABLY THE WORLD'S most popular pet is the cat. From the most ancient times, the supple, clean little animal has delighted and awed man. Almost every culture has accepted the cat. Even in the Moslem world, where animals are generally ignored or despised, the cat enjoys a comfortable status. It is one of the few animals mentioned with approval in the Koran.

The European cat first appeared on that continent around 700 B.C. It was a cross between the sacred cat of Egypt (brought in by Phoenician traders) and the small European wildcat.

The new little crossbreed was quickly domesticated by the people of pre-Christian Europe. Many skeletons of these ancient pets have been found in the excavated ruins of Roman villas and town sites. Early English and Scottish documents also mention cats as household pets.

In pagan northern Europe the cat was revered as an attendant of Freya, the goddess of love. With the advent of Christianity, however, the once honored cat was scorned as a pagan symbol. In time, it also became feared as a guise for Satan and a companion of witches.

Cats suffered cruelly because of this superstition, and from others, as well. In medieval Europe, for instance, countless animals died because it was believed that a raging fire would be extinguished if a calico cat was thrown into the consuming flames.

Eventually, reason returned. The cat regained its popularity as a pet and was restored to its cozy place on the domestic hearth.

Sleek, clever, and independent, cats have always been associated with mystery. Because of this, they have been widely used as symbols of religion, from the long-haired temple cats of Tibet and Burma to the Lion of the Resurrection. Early Christians believed that the big cat's whelp was born dead and did not breathe until three days later.

Cats were highly regarded in ancient Egypt. They were sacred to Isis, goddess of the moon, and were objects of veneration. Anyone who killed a cat, even accidentally, was put to death. When a pet cat died, the owner had it embalmed and ceremoniously buried. Out of this grew a curious custom. Because no one would dare to desecrate the grave of a sacred cat, Egyptians often hid their valuables with the dead animal. It might be said that this was the beginning of the safe deposit box.

Cats, unlike dogs, are not working animals; you simply can't make a cat do anything. But there is one recorded instance when Tabby was put to work. That was in Paris at the end of the 1700s when a few silly women of fashion started a new fad—dancing to the music of a cats' chorus.

This "music" was provided by lining up a dozen or more cats under the raised lid of a clavichord, the fore-runner of the grand piano. The captive animals were placed so that their heads stuck out above the instrument while their tails hung down in back. By rhythmically twisting the dangling tails, the "music master" got from the unhappy cats a continuous response of hisses and howls. These combined to make the strangest medley of sound ever heard under the name of song. Happily for both cats and the world of music, this fad was short-lived.

"European Cat"   Poland, 1964

The Great Water Prairie

It is a region of mystery, wild beauty, and danger. In it grows the tree of death.

MOST OF SOUTH Florida is taken up by the world's most strangely beautiful region—the vast water prairie known as The Everglades.

Sometimes called a "river of grass," this great subtropical area is one hundred miles long and up to seventy miles wide. It is a mysterious world of cypress, lush hummocks, saw grass, ancient black muck, and silent water.

Within the shadowy protection of The Everglades safely roost some of the country's rarest and most beautiful birds—the egret, the roseate spoonbill, the great heron. Here too abounds the alligator, a reptile found nowhere else in the world except for a small corner in China.

The Everglades is a region hostile to man; he invades it but is rarely comfortable there. Only the Semiones have ever found it congenial. To this small, independent tribe, The Everglades have been home for centuries. They understand and love this strange world. In the disastrous war between the Seminoles and the United States (1835–1842), the great brooding swamp also proved a useful ally for the Indians. Under the leadership of their famous chief Osceola, many Seminoles survived to fight again by escaping their pursuers and hiding out in The Everglades' untrackable waste.

The eerie beauty of the great water prairie is unmatched anywhere, but it is also a place of many dangers. One of these is a leafy killer which lurks deep within this aqueous world.

It is the manchineel, the most poisonous tree on the North American continent. Every part of this tree is malignant, its fruit and its sap, its foliage and its bark. So evil is its reputation that even its very shade was once thought to be fatal.

Indians call the manchineel "Tree of Death," and once they tipped the penetrating ends of their war arrows with its virulent milky-white sap. When the exploring Spaniards arrived in the New World, they found the manchineel growing in abundance beside the swamps and tidewaters of south Florida. Bitter encounters with the death-dealing tree soon taught the newcomers to fear it. So they began systematically to exterminate the green menace wherever they came upon it.

The Spaniards also gave the tree its present name, which is derived from their word for "little apple." The name referred to the manchineel's fruit, which is small and looks something like a crabapple—yellow, smooth, and rosy-cheeked when ripe. But right there the similarity ends. The fruit of the manchineel is deadly; within its firm white flesh it harbors a powerful alkaloid.

When the "apple" is eaten, this poison acts quickly to bring on severe vomiting, excruciating abdominal pains, and internal hemorrhage. The terrible seizure generally ends in death. Even small amounts of the fruit can cause bleeding stomach ulcers.

The sap is equally vicious and very destructive to mucous membranes. A touch of it to the mouth can cause serious lesions. And blindness has resulted when some of the sap has been accidentally rubbed into the soft, moist tissue of the eyes. Contact with the highly toxic bark or leaves of the manchineel produces painful red welts and sores on the skin.

Early settlers, seeking to eliminate the manchineel, found that they could not cut down the harmful tree by the usual means. Whenever a woodsman drove his axe into the tree's reddish-brown bark, he was immediately sprayed by its caustic sap. Later, the settlers learned to burn the tree and "draw its poison" before felling it. But great care was then taken to avoid the poison-laden smoke.

In the 1950s, Dr. Werner H. Lauter, a chemist from the University of Florida, carried out extensive field and laboratory studies on this uniquely savage tree. Twice during his research in the Everglades the doctor was a victim of the manchineel's virulence. Once, a few drops of rainwater falling from a leaf caused severe blistering of his ear. Later, while he was doing laboratory work on the "little apple," a drop of the fruit's juice squeezed through a pinpoint hole in one of Dr. Lauter's rubber gloves. In a short time, his arm was covered with angry skin ulcers and temporarily paralyzed.

The "Tree of Death" gives no outward sign of its threatening nature. A distant cousin of the lovely poinsettia, the manchineel is pleasingly round and bushy in contour. Its average height is about twenty feet, although it may grow taller.

The fruit of the manchineel appears quite innocent and is not unpleasant to taste or smell. There are references to its attractiveness, especially for the children of early settlers. Free to roam the virgin woods and to eat off the land, the unwary youngsters were often the victims of the lethal "little apple."

Today, few people will ever suffer poisoning by the manchineel. Centuries of extermination have almost eliminated the toxic tree. Almost the only place it is found now is in the deepest recesses of The Everglades, in silent swamps rarely visited by man.

Isolation has eliminated the tree's dangers. In the United States, there are more than ten thousand cases of plant poisonings reported each year, many of them fatal. Ironically, for several years not a single one of these cases has been caused by the nation's most potent arboreal poisoner, the once-dreaded manchineel.

"The Everglades"   U.S.A., 1947

In the Land of the Reindeer

They were first to feel the lasso—and they can float on their own hair.

DAG HAMMARSKJÖLD ONCE said that the life of Lapland is "tied to the ancient rhythm of reindeer breeding."

The reindeer, to the Arctic Lapp, is his most vital possession, providing him with transportation, food, clothing, bone utensils, even medicine in the form of powdered antlers.

The herding of reindeer has made a nomad of the Lapp, forcing him to follow his animals endlessly as they roam the vast silent tundra and coastal mountains in search of fresh vegetation to feed on, or to escape from the pestilential mosquitoes.

Once a year the Lapp rounds up his herd. I have

been in Swedish Lapland during one of these reindeer roundups. That's when all the foraging animals scattered over a particular area are gathered together and driven into a huge public corral made of logs and wire. Once all the reindeer are inside the corral (some of which hold thousands of milling animals), the big gates to the enclosure are slammed shut and the Lapps climb in to separate their own reindeer from those of their fellow herders.

The Lapps have no difficulty in picking out their own reindeer, easily identifying them by means of a "branding" notch cut into the animals' ears at birth. As soon as a herder spots one of his own deer, he sends his lasso singing through the air, captures the bucking animal neatly around its branching antlers, and then leads it off to one of the small corrals reserved for the individual herds. The annual roundup is the only means by which a Lapp can make an accurate check of his roving stock.

The reindeer may be the first animal ever to have felt the tightening restraint of the lasso, as the Lapps were using the rope for herding purposes centures before our West was discovered. One of the earliest mentions of reindeer herding was made in a ninth-century letter written by Norway's King Ottar to Alfred the Great of England. In the letter, Ottar spoke of his fine herd of six hundred animals.

It was also in Norway that reindeer had their finest hour when one of their number appeared briefly on the stage of history. Galloping dauntlessly through ice and snow for two solid days, this historic animal carried a messenger safely to the king with a warning that saved the nation. Having done his duty, and overcome by the strain of prolonged and speedy travel, the reindeer promptly dropped dead in the palace yard. A portrait of the antlered patriot may be seen today in the museum at Trondheim.

It is estimated that about 300,000 reindeer, most of them in domestic herds, roam over the European Arctic of Finland, Sweden, and Norway. About two million more are said to live on the Eurasian tundra, which includes Siberia.

Alaska actually has more reindeer than European Lapland. A count made some years ago placed the number in our largest state at over 700,000.

Reindeer are not native to North America, and the flourishing community of Santa's helpers in Alaska dates back only to 1891 when an American missionary, Dr. Sheldon Jackson, imported a herd of sixteen animals from Siberia. He hoped, by this means, to help the Eskimos supplement their dwindling supply of seal meat. The minister's experiment was a success, and reindeer raising supports many native Alaskans today.

A reindeer can never make a sneak attack. Due to a curious tendon in his ankle, he clicks when he walks like a mad Spanish dancer with castanets.

His rough hide is covered with coarse hair which he never sheds. Each hair is like a tiny air-filled tube which makes him so buoyant in the water he is able to swim with most of his body above the surface.

Unlike other antlered animals, there is no double standard among reindeer; the female as well as the male sports a multipronged headpiece. In the male, however, the antlers are larger and have more points, sometimes as many as sixty.

One of the reindeer's worst natural enemies is the northern raven, who swoops down on unattended newborn calves and kills them by pecking out their eyes.

In snowy Finland, reindeer-drawn sleds are a common means of getting around. To meet the hazards of increasing traffic, the first official reindeer-driver's school was opened at Pohtimolampi in Finnish Lapland. To get his license, a prospective driver must demonstrate that he can manage with only one rein, not fall out of the tipsy "pulkka" (sled to you), and get the reindeer to stop, which is not easy.

Finland was also the first country ever to penalize a man for drunken reindeer-driving. In 1956, a man in the little town of Kittela was fined thirty dollars for this strange traffic violation.

The new license notes the possibility of drunken reindeer-drivers, and warns that they face the same punishment as do boozy drivers of cars.

"Reindeer"   Finland, 1960

The Pilgrims' Savior

The remarkable Indian brave surprised the
Pilgrims by greeting them in English.

WHEN THAT BRAVE little band of fifty Pilgrim survivors
counted their blessings on that long-gone autumn day
in 1621, the name of Squanto must have been frequently on their lips, for without the most remarkable
Indian of his time, there could have been no Thanksgiving Day that first year—nor, perhaps, even a Plymouth Colony.

It was Squanto, out of his strange devotion to the
Pilgrims, who had told them when to plant the un-
familiar corn and how to fertilize it with fish heads.
It was Squanto who showed them how to track game
and led them to streams where the fish ran best.

Above all, it was Squanto who insured the safety

of the struggling little colony by arranging a peace treaty with the powerful Massasoit, chief of the Wampanoags. Without such a treaty, the Pilgrims could not have survived; hostile Indians would have wiped them out.

When the Pilgrims landed on the rocky coast of Massachusetts in December of 1620, Squanto had already made four voyages across the Atlantic, had learned to speak fluent English and Spanish, and had been converted to Christianity. He was familiar with the comforts of English living, had seen the ancient grandeur of Spain, and personally knew several of the great explorers of that day.

Squanto's adventures began in 1605 when, as a handsome young brave of the Pawtuxet tribe, he was captured by George Weymouth, an English explorer who was mapping the unknown coast of Massachusetts.

The "New World savages," as the Indians were then called, were still a rarity in Europe, although from the time of Columbus explorers had frequently brought them back to the Continent. Sometimes they were exhibited, but more often they were attached to the retinues of the wealthy. Such Indians were generally treated well in England, and Squanto was no exception. But although he lived there for some years, he never ceased yearning for his own people, and eventually he was sent back to Massachusetts aboard a vessel under the command of Captain John Smith, the gentleman best remembered because Pocahontas intervened to save his life. When the expedition reached the New England coast in 1614, Squanto bid Smith farewell and left the ship to rejoin his tribe.

He was not to remain with his own people for very long. In that same year, he and twenty-seven other Pawtuxet braves were lured aboard the ship of an English adventurer, Captain John Hunt. They were put in chains and taken to the Spanish port of Malaga, where there was a large and active slave market. There the treacherous Hunt sold all his young Indian captives.

By a stroke of luck, Squanto was bought by a monk who abhorred slavery. The kindly man took the unhappy Indian to a monastery, nursed him back to health, and instructed him in Spanish and the Christian faith.

Freed by the monks, Squanto managed to get to England. There, in 1619, through the kind efforts of an officer in the powerful Newfoundland Trading Company, Squanto was put aboard an outbound ship and returned, once again, to his homeland near Cape Cod.

But now a terrible shock was in store for the weary Indian. When he at last reached his native village, he was met with the stony silence of desolation. His ancestral village stood in ruins, the people gone, all wiped out by a plague which had swept through the tribe a few years earlier. Of all the Pawtuxets who had ever lived, only Squanto, the unwilling wanderer, survived.

Heartbroken and homeless, Squanto went to live with the people of Chief Massasoit, the Wampanoags, a great tribe of hunters whose village was also on the Massachusetts shore. And he was still living with the Wampanoags when, in December of the following year, the little band of Pilgrims came ashore to establish the first permanent European settlement in the wilderness that was New England.

Squanto and the Pilgrims met for the first time early the next spring, and from the beginning this English-speaking, Christian "savage"—whom the Pilgrims later called "saint"—attached himself to the settlers, preferring their company even over that of his own people.

Squanto's strong, gentle character, his skill at hunting and husbandry, all worked to convince the Pilgrims that he was Heaven-sent, that the appearance of this extraordinary Indian among them was providential. Even William Bradford, the hardheaded, sternly devout leader of the Plymouth Colony, said that he believed Squanto had been sent as a "special instrument of God for (our) good."

Squanto's friendship for the Pilgrims, however, was not without risk. One of Squanto's greatest services had been to act as their interpreter to the surrounding Indians. Most of these had accepted Squanto's role as "the white man's tongue," but a small band of warlike Indians living out on Cape Cod distrusted him for this skill.

Determined to get rid of Squanto, they prepared an ambush, captured him, and sentenced him to death. Before they could carry out the execution, however, the colony learned of Squanto's fate and Miles Standish, captain of the settlement's tiny "army," marched out to attack the hostile Indians, routed them, and rescued Squanto.

Although Squanto did not forfeit his life for his friends then, he did die in their service later. In 1622, while acting as guide to Governor Bradford on an exploring expedition, Squanto fell sick and died, probably of pneumonia.

No monument marks Squanto's unknown burial place, and history scarcely mentions his name, but if one man above all others might be said to be responsible for that first Feast of Thanksgiving, then that man would surely be Squanto, the Indian brave who became "the Pilgrims' saint."

"Landing of the Pilgrims" U.S.A., 1970

The Case of the
Dutchman's Leg

Which leg did Peter Stuyvesant have
amputated—and whatever happened to
it?

ON MAY 11, 1647, Peter Stuyvesant, the last Dutch
governor to rule the New World colony known as the
New Netherlands, first set foot on the island of Manhattan. For almost three hundred years afterward, the
question was—which foot?

A peg leg had replaced one of his sturdy living ones
in March, 1644, when Stuyvesant, then governor of the
Dutch Windward Islands and stationed on Curaçao,
mounted an attack against the Spanish defenders of St.
Martin. The offensive fizzled, and Stuyvesant's only
significant military act during the encounter was to
stop a Spanish cannonball, which shattered his leg.

The wooden leg with which Stuyvesant was later

equipped, however, was to prove something of a continuing mystery. The riddle of Peter's leg commenced with his death. Some years before that, while he was still governor of New Amsterdam, Stuyvesant had acquired a magnificent estate on New York's Bowery, to which he retired after the surrender of New Amsterdam to the British in 1664. Peter died there in 1672 and, in a modest ceremony, was laid to rest in a huge vault beneath a small private chapel he had built on his estate in 1660. With him into the grave went the answers to two questions that were to plague artists, historians, and monument makers for generations:

1. Although mention of Stuyvesant's injury had frequently been made in the correspondence and official records of that day, which leg had he lost? Some said the right, others the left.

2. Where had the amputation taken place—on St. Martin; in Curaçao; or at the medical school at Leyden University, in Holland, where it was known that Stuyvesant had been fitted with a wooden leg many months after the disastrous battle in the Caribbean?

The question of which leg became fair play for anybody's guess, and eventually there came into being a host of paintings and statues depicting the dead governor with either the right leg or the left missing, depending on which authority the artist had relied upon. One artist, unable to make any decision, had painted a pre-St. Martin's Stuyvesant planted firmly on two good legs!

In time, the answer to the first of these vexing questions finally came—and from the old governor himself.

In 1799, Stuyvesant's private chapel had been replaced with a handsome church which was built over the burial vault and is famous today as St. Mark's In The Bowery. It is now the oldest place of continuous worship in New York. In the early part of this century it became evident that extensive repairs would have to be made on the damp and sagging crypt beneath the church. As the vault had to be thrown open to the workmen, it seemed to the churchmen at St. Mark's an excellent opportunity to go a step further and settle, once and for all, the question of which leg "Peter the Headstrong" had lost from that fateful cannonball.

So the lid of the moldered coffin was gently prized open and the answer irrefutably given—the occupant, in a fine state of preservation, was found to be minus his right leg, just below the knee.

However, there still remained the question of just where Stuyvesant's leg had been amputated after the original injury. Several years ago, while I was in Curaçao, I decided to check up on this. After considerable research, I found that the wounded Stuyvesant, following his unfortunate encounter on St. Martin's, had been brought back to Curaçao for the amputation.

The severance must have been a nightmare. The surgeons of those days were still actually nothing more than barbers with leeches and hacksaws, men more skilled in shaping beards than in separating limbs from still-living bodies. That Stuyvesant survived this terrible ordeal is a testament to his strength and determination.

But the most amazing disclosure, to me, was the treatment accorded the amputated leg itself. It was the custom in those days that when a man lost a leg or an arm, the severed member was given a formal "Christian" burial. Stuyvesant's leg received a full military funeral. With banners waving and drums beating a doleful tattoo, it was carried in a small coffin to a little graveyard just outside the great walls of the Dutch fort. There the leg was laid to rest amid ceremonies far more elaborate than those which marked the passing of the man himself twenty-eight years later!

The graveyard may still be visited in Curaçao. It is now a delightful little park called Wilhelmina in honor of the old Dutch queen.

"Peter Stuyvesant, Volunteer Fireman"   U.S.A., 1948

Sybil Ludington

She's the girl who outrode Paul Revere.

THANKS TO LONGFELLOW'S poem, "hardly a man is now alive" who doesn't know about Paul Revere's "famous ride." Revere's place in history is secure, and rightfully so, as his work that night was the work of a patriot.

But who knows about the courageous sixteen-year-old girl who actually outrode Paul Revere to alert the countryside that "the British are coming"?

This Revolutionary heroine was Sybil Ludington, the daughter of a prosperous Putnam County, New York, landowner who was also colonel of the local Minute-men. Like Ludington, these were all farmers who stood armed and ready to defend their homes against any surprise attack by the British.

On the night of April 27, 1777, the attack came. An exhausted Minuteman courier brought the news from nearby Danbury to Ludington.

"The British have landed from Long Island Sound and are attacking in force," gasped the horseman, spent with hard riding. "They have orders to sweep the countryside and destroy all our weapons and stores. All who resist will be shot at once. They have already overrun Danbury and burnt it to the ground. Now they are headed this way.

"And," the rider added, "they are dangerous, all drunk on rum."

Colonel Ludington lost no time in making his decision; every Minuteman must be called out to fight at once. But Ludington could not leave to round them up. His farm was the point at which the Minutemen were to muster and form ranks to meet the advancing British. Nor could the courier round up the armed farmers; the man was so tired he could hardly keep in his saddle.

It was then that Sybil stepped forward. She would go. She knew all the farmers, knew every inch of the countryside, and she could handle a horse well. Just let her ride out, she pleaded to her father, and she would have all available men at the Ludington farm before first light.

It was a dangerous mission for a young girl, but Ludington had no choice. Reluctantly, he gave his consent.

A big farm horse was led from the stable and, wrapped in a warm cloak and carrying a cudgel-like stick, Sybil was on the animal's back at once. Calling good-bye to those who stood in the lantern-lit farmyard, the girl flew off into the silent darkness.

All through the long night Sybil rode at a gallop, pressing herself and her horse on tirelessly. Hour after hour the girl sped through dozens of villages, past hundreds of farmhouses, pausing only to pull in her reins briefly as she came up to each night-barred door. Then, bending down from the back of her lathered horse, she thudded her heavy stick wildly against the resounding wood and shouted out the alarm:

"The British are on the march! Every man turn out! Every man turn out and fight!"

And the men of Putnam did just that. Heeding Sybil's call to arms, those "embattled farmers" mustered out in force and under the command of Colonel Ludington they not only stopped two thousand British regulars but drove them all the way back to their boats in defeat.

Teenage Sybil's courageous ride that night parallels Revere's in both its patriotic purpose and its outcome. But there were some differences and these mark Sybil's ride as far more difficult than Paul's.

Revere started his ride from the Charlestown side of Boston at about one hour before midnight. From there he raced twelve miles to Lexington where he stopped to warn Adams and Hancock, the rebel leaders who were then in hiding from the British. A conference was held among the men, after which Revere had supper and again set out on his ride to warn the town of Concord.

But Revere never reached Concord. He was stopped by a British patrol a mile outside Lexington. There, at about two o'clock in the morning, his ride came to an abrupt end when the British arrested him and confiscated his horse.

Paul Revere was carried on his famous mission by a fine riding horse that was saddled to perfection, he sped over roads which were excellent by the standards of that time, and he had the lights of a well-populated area to guide him.

In all, Revere traveled less than fourteen miles on that historic night and was actually in the saddle for only two hours.

Sybil, on the other hand, had only a big, ungainly farm horse for her mount and rode with the crudest equipment. She did not travel over good roads but floundered along cart tracks and rutted fields in the pitchy blackness of sleeping farmlands. Yet this brave, bright, and pretty girl rode the entire night through without dismounting, and she covered on her desperate gallop the staggering distance of more than forty miles!

There now exists a memorial to this young heroine of the American Revolution. It is a superb life-size bronze executed several years ago by the great sculptress, Anna Hyatt Huntington. It stands beside a lake in Putnam County, New York, and shows Sybil side-seated on a galloping horse, her upraised hand holding a cudgel, and her hair blowing wildly in the night wind.

"Sybil Ludington"   U.S.A., 1975

Fort Navidad

At the first celebration of Christmas in the
New World, they sang His praises in Latin.

ON THE NIGHT of Christmas Eve, 1492, Christopher
Columbus turned the helm of his flagship, the *Santa
Maria,* over to the hands of a fourteen-year-old deck
boy.

This was an unusual procedure for the admiral of the
Ocean Sea, but at the time the blue-black Caribbean
sky was clear, the sea calm, and the passage set for
straight ahead. The boy, who had some previous experience as a helmsman, could certainly be trusted
under such circumstances to keep the graceful caravel
on course. Besides, Columbus and his men were all
badly in need of sleep.

A few hours later, just on midnight, as the bells in

far-away Spain commenced to ring in the new Christmas
day, the *Santa Maria* ran aground and broke up on a
shallow reef near what is now Cap-Haitien, on the north
coast of Haiti.

The loss of the *Santa Maria* created a serious seagoing housing problem as the surviving vessels, the *Nina*
and *Pinta,* were too small to accommodate all the ship-
wrecked seamen who now needed shelter. So Columbus
gave orders for his men to salvage all the available
timbers from the wrecked flagship and use the wood to
build a small fort on shore. This would protect them
from both the weather and attacks by possibly hostile
Indians.

The fort was a crude structure, put up in haste by
very weary men, but it was to have a significance far
beyond anything ever dreamed of by its builders. It was
to be the very first building erected by Europeans in
the New World, and within its walls of shattered timbers would be held the first celebration of Christmas on
this continent.

Columbus named the little fort "Navidad," the Spanish word for the Nativity. And in Fort Navidad that
first day a Christmas mass was sung by the three ships'
officers and men, devout worshippers all.

Although no precise record exists of that first service,
it is believed that it included the ancient Christmas song
the "Angelic Hymn," familiar to us today as the deeply
moving "Angels We Have Heard on High." With its
soaring refrain of "Gloria in Excelsis Deo" rising on the
alien air, the hymn would give new hope to that little
band of men who, that day, stood utterly alone on the
edge of a vast and secret land.

I first learned about Fort Navidad—"Fort Christmas"—when I went to Haiti several years ago to get
the story of Hurricane Hazel, the murderous storm
which had raked the island shortly before.

One day I flew over to Cap-Haitien from Port-au-Prince with a Haitian friend, a member of the government. We set down near the small seaside village and he pointed out to me a grass-covered mound that lay close to the water. Then he told me the story of the fort as I have told it here.

Of course, the makeshift fort itself is totally gone. The remnants of its ancient rotted timbers are now buried deep within the earth of centuries.

Strangely, not far away was to be seen another historic Haitian fort, also created by a man claiming the name of Christopher. It was the Citadel, the great fortress built more than a century and a half ago by Haiti's tyrant emperor, Henri Christophe. Crowning the sheer towering peak known as the Bishop's Bonnet, the Citadel is a stunning engineering feat, the black man's greatest architectural achievement and a marvel among all manmade wonders anywhere in the world.

But while I viewed the mighty fortress with awe, I was touched by the little lost fort.

So when I returned to New York I did some research on it and finally came up with a rough sketch of Fort Navidad which had been made by Columbus himself. The sketch was included in a letter to the treasurer of the king of Spain. Columbus had written him this letter in March, 1493, while the great navigator was returning from the New World aboard the *Nina*.

Previously I had designed some stamps for foreign governments, and I thought Columbus's sketch of the little fort would make a fine stamp for Haiti. It could be a special Christmas issue with the proceeds going to aid the victims of Hurricane Hazel.

This suggestion was accepted by the Haitian government, and the stamp design was immediately made up in New York. The American Bank Note Company did the printing and the stamps—airmail and surface denominations—were sold through the Haitian post office that following Christmas. My own Christmas card that year used the special stamp on the first day of issue.

It seemed a fitting way to honor that brave little band of men who celebrated the first Christmas in the New World almost half a thousand years ago.

"Fort Navidad"   Haiti, 1954

There She Waves

Special permission is needed to fly one
American flag in Holland.

U.S. FLAG 1795-1818 (FT. McHENRY FLAG)

WHEN FRANCIS SCOTT KEY watched the bombardment
of Fort McHenry on that historic night in 1814, he had
no trouble seeing the flag that was to inspire our national
anthem. It was the largest flag of its time.

The fort's flag had been made extra large in defiance
of the advancing British enemy. Stitched together hurriedly by three Baltimore women, the banner had fifteen
stars and fifteen bars, and measured thirty by forty-
two feet.

The separate sections of the flag were so big they
could not be joined to each other in the small house
in which they were made. So they were taken to the

long malt room of a neighboring brewery and there assembled into the finished flag.

Since that time, flags have grown larger and larger. The largest in the world today is the American flag which hangs from a Detroit department store. It is a staggering 104 feet by 235 feet and weighs in at 1,500 pounds. A battery of workmen equipped with winches and hoists are required to set the giant standard in place, a job not without danger.

Hauling down a small flag can also be dangerous. In fact, a man once died for just such a simple act.

In 1862, when the Union forces took the city of New Orleans, they raised the Stars and Stripes above a building which had formerly been a branch of the United States Mint.

A passionate young Southerner, bitter at the defeat of the city's Confederate defenders, immediately climbed the pole and tore the hated Northern symbol down.

A Union search for the man ensued, and a protesting youth was quickly seized. Just as quickly, he was tried, found guilty, and hanged by a military court.

It was a tragic incident in an emotional war, but it was made doubly tragic when it was discovered later that the wrong man had been executed. The boy who had actually torn down the flag had escaped from New Orleans, joined the Confederate Army, and soon after died in battle.

But not all affronts to the flag committed during the heat of the Civil War had such somber endings.

A Maryland woman, a staunch Confederate, loudly and publicly proclaimed her joy over the death of Abraham Lincoln, and refused to display the Stars and Stripes in mourning (as had been ordered by the Union military authorities). She was quickly warned that unless she changed her mind and flew the flag within twenty-four hours, she would face a long prison term.

Unable to find a flag anywhere, the angry woman was forced to buy the needed cloth and make her own. Working at top speed to meet the time limit, she finally completed the flag right down to its last difficult five-pointed star. She was not happy to fly it, but she knew she would be considerably less happy languishing in prison.

The most unusual incident concerning handmade flags occurred when President Eisenhower made his official visit to India.

New Delhi, the capital of the host country, found to its great embarrassment that there were only a few American flags on hand for use in honoring the president. It was too late and too costly to buy the great number of banners needed to decorate the city, so the government turned to its people for help.

At that time, hundreds of poor families around New Delhi were engaged in a program to help support themselves by producing handmade articles in their own homes. So the government brought carloads of native thread to these "cottage workers" and they immediately went to work on the flags.

In less than two weeks, these skillful men and women had woven the cotton thread into cloth, dyed it red, white, and blue, and then had cut and stitched it into more than twenty-five thousand handsome American flags.

I have one of these flags, which was given to me on a news-gathering visit I made to India at that time. In my opinion, the Stars and Stripes has never received from any foreign nation a warmer tribute than this one from the "cottage workers" of India.

One of the most costly American flags never flew. In 1966, a London collector paid $16,200 for the pattern

of a United States flag which showed a design that wa.
never approved. The unique flag had the usual thirteer
stripes, but the thirty-seven stars in its field of blue wer(
in a diamond and side bar arrangement. The flag hac
been designed immediately after the Civil War ended
and the pattern was presented to President Lincoln fo}
his approval in April, 1865. Three days later, he wa
assassinated and the new flag was never made.

We are all stirred by the sight of the country's flag.
but until recently this has been a feeling denied to
the blind. Now, however, The Daughters of the American Revolution have created a banner for the sightless.
This unusual flag was made to be "seen" by sensitive
hands. They can feel the rough felt of the red stripes,
the cool satin of the white stripes, and the embroidered
outlines of the stars on a heavy blue cotton ground.

One of the strangest uses of the flag may be found
in Holland. Over the huge building which houses the
international freight-forwarding firm of Wambersie and
Zoon in Rotterdam flies an 1820 American flag with
twenty stars. It is the Dutch company's official "house
flag." It has been used as such for a century and a half,
ever since the original Wambersie first went to Holland
as an American consul and stayed there to start the
mammoth firm. This is the only place in the world where
the flag is used in this way, and it is allowed only by
special permission from our State Department.

The most impressive, one-and-only use of our flag
is found in the Mount Olivet Cemetery in Frederick,
Maryland, and it marks a singular distinction. In all the
United States, there are only a few places where the
Stars and Stripes is allowed to fly twenty-four hours a

day, every day in the year. Of these, the only place where it is flown to honor a single man is in this cemetery, over the grave of Francis Scott Key, father of our national anthem.

"The Fort McHenry Flag"   *U.S.A., 1968*

The Bones of Santa Claus

The old saint's bones rest in three different cities.

In 1972, THE bones of Santa Claus came to the New World.

In a fine ecumenical gesture, the Roman Catholic archdiocese of Bari, Italy, gave to the Greek Orthodox archdiocese of New York several relics of Saint Nicholas of Myra—the gentle bishop whom we know best as the saint of Christmas.

The gift is a fitting one, as Saint Nicholas is the patron saint of both Bari and New York. The early Dutch settlers who bought Manhattan Island from the Indians believed that Saint Nicholas guided them in their purchase.

Among these sacred relics are several fragments of

bone from the saint's skull, a small vial of myrrh exuded from his bones, some cloth from his winding sheet, and a piece of wood from a coffin which once held his remains. All these have been placed in a beautiful jeweled reliquary and are now enshrined in the new Greek Orthodox Church of Saint Nicholas in Flushing, a residential area of New York City.

This means that the bones of Saint Nicholas now rest in three separate places, continents apart: in the Mideast, in Europe, in the United States.

But in the ancient church at Myra (now Demre, Turkey) where Saint Nicholas served as bishop and where he was buried over sixteen hundred years ago, his original tomb stands empty, a gaping hole in its marble side. No part of the saint remains there.

How did all this come about? Well, it's a fascinating story and one which I came upon firsthand several years ago. At that time, I had just learned that the Turkish government was restoring the ruined fourth-century church of Saint Nicholas at Demre. I was surprised that a Moslem country would make such a restoration. It seemed to be an unusual act of goodwill, and I thought that others might like to know about it also.

Previously I had designed a few foreign stamps. Now I designed one showing Saint Nicholas and his ancient church and presented it for approval to the Turkish government. The design was well received, and it appeared on a stamp which Turkey issued just in time for the holidays. What makes the stamp unique is that it was issued by a Moslem country to commemorate a Christian shrine.

The ancient church which appears on the stamp is where Saint Nicholas served as bishop early in the fourth century. The church was built in the Greco-Roman style and was quite imposing. However, it also turned out to be a very difficult project for restoration. There had been a long, steady silting over of the entire coast around Myra, and most of the old stone structure had sunk below the surrounding land level.

Actually, it had become a subterranean church, but despite this it remained open. Over the centuries, small bands of worshippers—often in fear of their lives—had worked to keep the interior of the church clear of the alluvial deposits which had slowly engulfed the massive outer walls.

A flight of worn stones leads down into the ancient church to the altar where Saint Nicholas once celebrated mass. Around the altar is a kind of mini-amphitheater of stone benches, a seating arrangement often found in early Christian churches. Opening off the nave are two broad aisles. In one of these stands the mutilated sarcophagus which once held the saint's body.

The man who was to become Saint Nicholas—according to the scanty records available—was born in Patara, in Biblical Asia Minor (now Turkey), some time late in the third century. The city, then under Roman rule, was a busy port on the Mediterranean and is mentioned in the New Testament in connection with a missionary voyage undertaken by Saint Paul. Today, Patara is gone. Now called Gelemis, its harbor has been silted out of existence and the city itself reduced to an obscure village.

The parents of Saint Nicholas were a well-to-do couple who died early and left their young son a considerable fortune. But the youth's only interest in money was to use it for relief of the poor. He was already a devout Christian, like many of his friends. Asia Minor was an early seedbed for Christianity, and those who embraced the vigorous new faith practiced it with selfless ardor.

Like other early Christians, Saint Nicholas suffered some religious persecution under the intolerant Roman emperor Diocletian. But this ceased under the succeeding emperor, Constantine, who made Christian worship lawful.

Some time during his young manhood, as an act of Christian faith, Saint Nicholas made a pilgrimage from Patara to Jerusalem. After his visit to the Holy City, Saint Nicholas returned to Asia Minor, but not to his home in Patara. Instead, he settled in Myra (now Demre), which was another port city about forty miles eastward along the coast.

Why he did this is not known. But Myra was then already the seat of the bishopric and he may have found the religious atmosphere of the town congenial to his devout nature.

There is no exact record of just when Saint Nicholas became bishop of Myra, but there is evidence that he was one of the powerful clergymen who attended the first great ecumenical Council of Nicaea (now Iznik, Turkey) in 325 A.D.

Saint Nicholas had a deep love of children and is known to have performed many acts of kindness toward them. He is their patron saint, although he is called by several different names. To us, he has come down as Santa Claus. This is a corruption of his Dutch name, Sinterklass.

He is the patron saint of sailors, too, and on their behalf is credited with many miracles at sea. Pawnbrokers and thieves have also sought refuge beneath the mantle of his holy protection.

When Saint Nicholas died (his death date is given variously from 326 to 342 A.D.) he was laid to rest in a handsome marble crypt at Myra. There he slept peacefully for seven centuries while his church slowly sank beneath the encroaching silt and the world around his tomb changed from Roman to Moslem.

Then, in 1087, the quiet of his grave was shattered. In that year the people of Bari, a port on Italy's Adriatic coast, mounted an expedition to Asia Minor. Its purpose was to seize the hallowed bones of Saint Nicholas from the conquering Moslems who then held the old church. Saint Nicholas was the patron saint of Bari's seagoing population and they found it intolerable that their holy protector's remains should be in the hands of the infidel.

So forty-seven sailors and two priests sailed from Bari to Myra, made a surprise raid from the sea, gained entrance to the church, broke open the tomb of Saint Nicholas, and triumphantly carried his stolen bones back to Italy.

But they did not return to Bari with all the saint's bones. In their haste to get away safely they left some behind in the crypt. Today these bones, along with several other relics found later in and around the broken tomb, may be seen in the museum at Antalya, the provincial Turkish capital near Demre.

In Italy, the bones of Saint Nicholas were enshrined in a church built especially to honor them. They now lie in a handsome crypt beneath the altar of Bari's ancient Basilica of Saint Nicholas. Above the tomb flickers a solitary soft light. It comes from a little silver lamp shaped like a ship, the flame of which is perpetually fed by oils from both Italy and Asia. The ship is to remind us that Saint Nicholas is the patron saint of sailors, the oil from Asia is to signify his Eastern origin.

The bones of Saint Nicholas are precious relics for the faithful, but his spirit belongs to the world. There is no single other symbol of goodwill so widely accepted by all people everywhere as Santa Claus.

It's nice to know, too, that this Christmas saint really lived and that not only here, but in Moslem Turkey as well, a parent may tell a child: *"Evet, Virginya, Noel Baba Vardir."* Which means, of course . . . "Yes, Virginia, there is a Santa Claus."

"Saint Nicholas and the Church at Myra"   *Turkey, 1955*

Christmas Night on the Delaware, 1776

A victory was needed to boost morale.

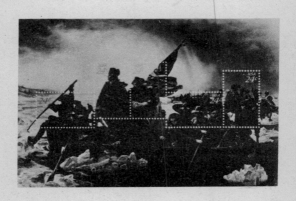

WHEN GEORGE WASHINGTON led his ragged troops across the Delaware River on Christmas night, 1776, he had only one thing on his mind: he was determined to gain a victory over the British.

And he did. He surrounded Trenton and beat the Hessian mercenaries there. Then he marched on to Princeton and trounced another British force. These successful actions, coming after his army's long retreat from New York, proved a much needed morale booster for the dispirited colonies.

In addition to his victories, Washington unwittingly did something more on that blustery night; he provided the inspiration for the most famous of all our historical paintings. It is, of course, *Washington Crossing the Delaware,* by the German-born artist Emmanuel Leutze.

(Another of Leutze's monumental paintings, *Westward the Course of Empire Takes Its Way,* may be seen in the Capitol; it hangs above the grand staircase in the House of Representatives.)

Leutze, who was born in 1816, came to this country as a boy with his immigrant parents. He began his art education in Philadelphia and then returned to Germany in 1841 for further study.

The artist remained in Germany for almost twenty years. During that time he started on a series of huge historical canvases dealing with American subjects. Among these was *Washington Crossing the Delaware.*

In his painting, Leutze used many of the subjects surrounding him as models. The boat in which Washington stands, for instance, is a Rhenish wine boat. The ice floes shown were those seen by the artist as he studied the Rhine River.

Originally, the big (twenty-two-foot) canvas was commissioned by Congress in 1851 for the Capitol Rotunda. As it turned out, Leutze was to make two versions of *Washington Crossing the Delaware* and neither was ever to adorn the Capitol.

The first version of the painting was scorched in a studio fire. Leutze repaired this and entered it in a German exhibition. It won a gold medal, was sold, and eventually was hung in a Bremen museum. It remained there until 1942, when it was destroyed in an Allied bombing raid. Among the bombers were many of Washington's countrymen.

The second painting of *Washington Crossing the Delaware* was turned down by Congress, despite their previous request for it. This rejection was probably due, in part, to some of the public criticism which greeted the painting when it was first shown. Many

thought the canvas too theatrical. Others found
unrealistic. They argued that no sensible man—esp
cially one who stood six feet three inches—would eve
endanger his life by standing up in so small a boat o
such rough water.

And then there was the matter of the flag shown i
the painting. That flag was not created until a year afte
the Delaware crossing, in 1777. If Washington had ha
a flag on his little boat, it would have had to have bee
the Grand Union flag (created in 1775) with thirtee
bars and the crosses of Saint George and Saint Andre
on its blue field. Washington had flown this flag fror
his headquarters, and it had also been used by our littl
fleet on the Delaware.

After Congress rejected the painting, it was sold pri
vately and often put on public exhibition. Over the years
it gained great public acclaim and was finally acquire
by New York's Metropolitan Museum of Art.

Because of the painting's wide popular appeal and it
historical significance, the Metropolitan later transferre
the canvas, on extended loan, to the museum at Wash
ington Crossing State Park, in Pennsylvania. The parl
marks the place from which Washington mounted hi
invasion of New Jersey and crossed the Delaware t
victory on that long-ago Christmas night.

Today, this most beloved of all our national paint
ings is back at the Metropolitan, but it is not on displa
there—it will not be exhibited again until the Nev
American Wing is completed.

"Washington Crossing the Delaware" U.S.A., 1976

The World's Rarest Stamp

A mystery surrounded it for thirty years.

IT IS NOT much to look at, the world's rarest stamp. It's a one-cent black-on-magenta and it was issued by the British crown colony of Guiana in 1856. It is octagonal, pictures a sailing ship in its center, is crudely made and poorly colored. Among the irreverent, it is sometimes referred to as The Blob.

On the face of the stamp, in black ink, are the initials of E. D. Wright, assistant postmaster of Guiana when the stamp was issued. A Latin motto also appears on the stamp: "We Give and Seek in Return," it says. That's a pretty good hint to send out on a letter which you hope will bring back an answer.

The story of the British Guiana stamp is one of the

great sagas of the stamp world. For me nothing surpasses it in interest, not even the shocking tale of the two-cent Blue Hawaiian Missionary, a rare stamp for which one Paris philatelist murdered another in 1892.

The British Guiana came to light first in 1872. Vernon Vaughan, a schoolboy stamp collector living in the colony, found it among some old stamps in his attic. He thought it was too dreary looking and sold it to a friend for the equivalent of $1.50.

Several years later, the second boy sold his modest collection for $500 to a Liverpool stamp dealer named Thomas Ridpath. Checking out the collection, Ridpath spotted the dark-hued Guiana stamp as an unusual one and immediately sold it for a profit to Count Philippe von Ferrary, a wealthy Austrian philatelist living in France.

Ferrary, now the fourth owner of the stamp, kept it for more than forty years, until his death in 1917. The count had willed all his fabulous stamps to the Berlin Postal Museum, but this was not to be. After his death, the French government dubbed Ferrary an enemy alien and seized his collection as part payment for war reparations.

In 1923, France put Ferrary's entire collection up for auction. The British Guiana, now recognized as the world's rarest stamp, was bid on heavily, but it was finally knocked down to a rich American manufacturer, Arthur Hind, for $32,500.

In 1940, after Hind's death, the rare stamp went on the auction block for a second time. Again there was heavy international bidding for the famous one-cent stamp. And again it went to an American buyer . . . this time for $42,000.

But now something new was added. The celebrated stamp had been bought anonymously. An agent sworn to secrecy made the purchase and no one could find out the name of the owner.

For the next thirty years this wall of secrecy was never breached. Not even when the hidden owner, through an intermediary, allowed the stamp to be photographed. The only thing learned then was that the man's personal owner's "mark" was a comet. This appeared on the back of the stamp along with Ferrary's fleur-de-lis and Hind's clover leaf.

Then in 1970 the mysterious owner put his whole collection up for sale and his identity was at last disclosed. He was Frederick Small, a rich Australian businessman and philatelist living in Fort Lauderdale, Florida. Small had guarded his secret well. Not even his wife ever suspected that he owned the world's rarest stamp.

The Small collection, a very good one, brought in about $600,000 at two auctions. The British Guiana, of course, was the star of the show and, as expected, it brought the highest price ever paid for a postage stamp—$280,000. For the third time the winning bidder was an American, a noted stamp collector and dealer named Irwin Weinberg.

However, Weinberg did not buy the treasured stamp for himself. It was purchased as an investment by a Wilkes-Barre, Pennsylvania, syndicate. Like Small, the members of this joint venture did not care to identify themselves.

Although the syndicate still holds the stamp, its value has not stopped escalating. According to the authoritative *Scott's Catalogue,* the British Guiana is now worth a cool $325,000. And its value will continue to increase.

Unlovely, battered, frail, and more than a century old, this little piece of smudgy plum-red paper has nowhere to go but up. It is, after all, the only one of its kind in the world. And the only one of anything is always a priceless rarity.

The original rare stamp is shown here boxed on the modern stamp. Guyana is the present spelling for the South American republic that was once British Guiana, a colony of England.

"One-Penny British Guiana Commemorative"
Guyana, 1967